Women carpet weavers
in rural Turkey :
Patterns of employment,
earnings and status

Women, Work and Development, 15

Women carpet weavers in rural Turkey: Patterns of employment, earnings and status

Günseli Berik

International Labour Office   Geneva

ISBN 92-2-106004-7
ISSN 0253-2042

First published 1987

Printed in the German Democratic Republic   ZIM

PREFACE

Since the World Employment Conference in 1976, the ILO has given increasing attention to the working and living conditions of rural women. The Programme on Rural Women has comprised studies, advisory work, field projects, workshops and seminars, and exchange of experiences among developing countries. On the research side, one of the major themes pursued has been the investigation of the conditions of employment of women engaged in home-based production on a contractual basis. Case studies have already been carried out on lace and bidi making and the electronics industry.

The present study on women carpet weavers in rural Turkey provides another well-documented analysis of women's employment patterns in rural areas, and their status and roles. The study is based on field-work carried out by the author in 1983 in ten villages in rural Turkey. Handwoven carpets are a major export item for Turkey and carpet weaving represents a substantial share of income in rural areas, notably for poor and landless households. The author analyses successively the characteristics of carpet weaving employment, the economic position of the weaving household and the impact on the position of women workers.

Carpet weaving is an activity based on women's subordinate position in the household and the dependence of poor and landless households on weaving income. Merchants and exporters take advantage of these features of the rural weaving labour force. The remuneration is low, there are no social benefits and work is carried out under unhealthy conditions. The study shows how the women's contribution to household income is determined by the relation of production in weaving, household composition, and the prevailing agrarian and social structure. It demonstrates that a greater contribution from weaving to household income does not lead to greater financial autonomy for weavers, which is determined by women's position in the age and gender hierarchies of their household.

The study concludes with a discussion of measures necessary to bring about improvements in working conditions, social security benefits and earnings, and greater control by the producers over their incomes.

ACKNOWLEDGEMENTS

I should like to thank Cihan Bilginsoy, Carmen Diana Deere, James Kindahl and anonymous readers at the ILO for useful comments and suggestions on earlier drafts of this monograph. I am grateful to Münir Berik, Cihan Bilginsoy and Havva Kanyılmaz for accompanying me to villages on various visits. I express my thanks to the numerous women and men in the villages in Turkey, who hosted and assisted me, and put up with my constant questioning. Without their co-operation and help, this research could never have been realised. I also wish to thank the Rural Employment Policies Branch of the Employment and Development Department of the ILO for supporting this work.

CONTENTS

INTRODUCTION

In the last ten years, policy-oriented studies concerning women in development have emphasised the importance of women's participation in paid work as a way to improve their socio-economic position. This concern has led to the development of income-generating projects, most notably in handicrafts, for women in the Third World as a means of incorporating them into the development process and alleviating poverty. The basic assumption has been that by increasing women's participation in paid work, not only would the standard of living of women and their families increase, but women's social position would also improve. However, recent studies conducted in the Third World contest this position by showing that participation in paid work does not necessarily bring about an improvement in the status and roles of women and may indeed generate various contradictory effects on women's situation.

Turkey provides an example of a country in which women's employment and income-generating possibilities in handwoven carpet production have expanded since the early 1960s. The study analyses the effect of women's cash-generating activity on their gender position by examining the relations of production in carpet weaving and the factors that determine the economic contribution of rural carpet weavers to their households. It shows that the mere fact of engaging in paid work is insufficient to improve women's position. The impact of women's employment on their subordinate position in society is mediated by the characteristics of paid work: the mode of recruiting women for paid employment, the quality of work relations, practices in the workplace, and the magnitude of women's earnings. Moreover, the pre-existing social and ideological context and the agrarian structure are crucial in shaping this influence.

This study concurs with the proposition that participation in paid work generates contradictory effects on the subordination of women (Young, 1978; Benería and Sen, 1982; Elson and Pearson, 1981). In the words of Elson and Pearson, engaging in paid work could simultaneously "decompose" and "intensify" existing forms of sexual inequality, while at the same time "recomposing" new forms (1981, p. 157). Elson and Pearson note that while young women who work in factories producing for world markets are able to escape arranged marriages, this is accompanied by increased control over women's labour by fathers and the emergence of new forms of dependence on non-kin men. Arizpe and Aranda (1981) observe that in rural Mexico young women who engage in wage labour have a greater say in marriage

1

decisions, but enjoy only slightly increased personal consumption and continue to have limited physical mobility. These examples support the proposition that it may not be possible to draw a single conclusion as to the impact of paid work on women's position. They are also consistent with the conceptualisation of women's position as a category that entails various dimensions (Quinn, 1977; Whyte, 1978), with which this study concurs. Specifically, this study considers two aspects of the position of rural female carpet weavers - financial autonomy and women's control over their labour power - and shows that increased familial control over women's labour power accompanies greater financial autonomy of women.

In the following section the nature of carpet-weaving employment, the history of the carpet industry and research findings on women's position in rural Turkey are briefly reviewed. This is followed by a presentation of research objectives and the main hypotheses tested in the study. Finally, a brief description of the research method is presented.

Background on carpet-weaving employment and rural women's position

Carpet weaving is a predominantly home-based industry, mostly concentrated in rural areas of Turkey. The weavers are almost exclusively women. Although precise employment figures are not available, weavers constitute a significant share of female paid employment in rural areas. These weavers make cash contributions to household income, which in most cases are crucial for the subsistence of their households, and in a number of cases they generate funds which make household accumulation possible. Moreover, handwoven carpets constitute an important export item. In 1982 knotted carpets accounted for 3.8 per cent of the total export earnings and 13.9 per cent of the manufacturing export earnings of Turkey.[1]

The knotted carpet is a traditional handicraft. The large-scale production of export carpets in Anatolia in the late nineteenth century has been well documented (cf. Quataert, 1986). The industry, however, collapsed after the First World War and during the Great Depression in the 1930s, and remained dormant until the 1950s. The expansion of the economy in the 1960s and 1970s provided an impetus to the growth of carpet production. This meant that in some regions carpets that were traditionally woven for domestic use became commodities, and in other regions, commodity production began with the introduction of weaving.

Despite their important economic contribution to their households and to Turkey's export earnings, carpet weavers are not accounted for in national employment statistics. Moreover, they are absent from any official policy consideration. Their invisibility in policy-making and statistics can in large part be attributed to the nature of the employment. Weaving is a scattered form of employment carried out in homes and small rural workshops in thousands of villages, mostly concentrated in western and central Turkey. Carpets are woven under

2

three relations of production: independent household production, the putting-out system, and production in workshops. Today independent production accounts for the majority of total weaving employment in rural areas.

A second reason for the invisibility of weavers is that the activity is not seen as "work", and this results in the undervaluation of weaving labour. Three major reasons explain why carpet weavers working in both homes and workshops are not captured in national employment statistics.[2] First, rural weaving is almost always an activity carried out alongside agricultural work. Due to the absence of a formal structure of weaving work, women regard weaving activity as an integral part of their lives as "peasants", farmers and women, and do not consider themselves as "workers". Since census questions aim to record a single occupation, weavers are classified as unpaid family workers rather than counted as self-employed weavers or employees. Second, even if household members do not engage in agricultural production, where weaving is carried out at home the work is not considered as work, but as an activity that women take on to pass their "leisure" time. The work is interpreted as a leisure activity not only by census enumerators but also by male kin and the weavers themselves. Thirdly, weavers fear that taxes are or might be imposed on their earnings. In the case of workshop weavers, the social security contributions which must be borne by both the weaver and the employer are an immediate threat. Thus, even where weaving is a full-time activity, there are perceived advantages to concealing women's employment. Where weaving is undertaken at home with the use of family labour, the activity is exempt from income tax. However, weavers are either ignorant of the tax code or fear that an income tax might be introduced, and hence the activity is not reported.

Despite the absence of employment statistics, it is possible to estimate the importance of weaving employment. According to the 1980 Census, 18.8 per cent of employed women in Turkey work in paid employment, the rest being unpaid family workers (SIS, 1982). Women constitute 33.7 per cent of the economically active population but are heavily represented in the agriculture and animal husbandry sectors. In 1980, 84.6 per cent of economically active women worked in agriculture while only 40 per cent of men were in this sector. Moreover, 92.4 per cent of women who work in the agricultural sector are classified as unpaid family workers (SIS, 1982). As the nature of the underestimation of women's weaving work indicates, in census figures carpet weavers could have been classified in any category of economically active women or excluded from the labour force altogether. It is, therefore, misleading to express female weaving employment as a share of total female labour force or economically active women. Even with this caveat, estimates of the magnitude of employment in carpet weaving are revealing of its importance. Based on estimates of weaving employment for 1978 and 1981 reported in Celbiş (1979) and DPT (1982), we could estimate the number of carpet weavers in 1980 to be between 525,000 and 577,800. This figure corresponds to between

3.5 and 3.9 per cent of the total female labour force, or between 8 and 9 per cent of economically active women in 1980.

No systematic research on conditions of employment in carpet weaving in Turkey has been undertaken to date.[3] Moreover, research on rural women in Turkey is in its infancy.[4] Available research findings on rural women allow one to glimpse the different factors involved in the unequal social and economic position of women in the context of the changing household organisation and agrarian trans-formation. In general, relative to men, women in rural Turkey bear a disproportionately heavy workload, have limited decision-making power and access to schooling, spend less time and money on leisure acti-vities and on conspicuous consumption, and consume less food. While there are no time budget studies conducted in rural Turkey, case studies reveal the extensive tasks that rural women undertake and their disproportionate share in the overall workload (cf. Balaman, 1985, pp. 216-7; Kandiyoti, 1984; Özbay, 1982).

In rural Turkish society, patrilocality and patrilineality are the norm. The traditional peasant household is organised on the basis of the control of the oldest male over all household property and labour. Young women occupy the lowest position in the age and gender hierarchies in this household, performing the heaviest workload when they have the least prestige and power in the household. Women gain status as they age and bear (male) children, reaching their peak status when their sons bring daughters-in-law to the household. This stage corresponds to the lightest workload of their life cycle, when their work consists of supervising and organising the labour of young women. Thus, the patterns which govern women's position are similar to those of other Middle Eastern societies, with a woman's workload and status showing opposite trends over her life cycle (Dwyer, 1978).

Kandiyoti (1984) argues that the effects of agrarian trans-formation on the social organisation of the traditional peasant house-hold, and thus on women, vary by household economic position. She observes that in households with larger landholdings, which tend to be extended family households, agrarian transformation is associated with the retreat of women from agricultural production, while in small-holder and landless households it is associated with an intensifi-cation of women's workload. Agrarian transformation erodes the economic base of extended family households and brings about the gradual dissolution of the patrilocal extended family organisation among the smallholder and landless rural households. The trend towards nuclear households means that the workload is distributed among fewer women in the household, while the introduction of labour-intensive cash crops increases women's workload. Thus, a trade-off between workload and control over women appears to emerge. There is also evidence to suggest that, relative to their workload and compared to men, rural women derive an unequal share of the benefits of the extension of the cash nexus. Parallel to social and economic change, men's traditionally privileged position in rural society appears to be extended to new areas of decision-making and indeed reinforced (Kandiyoti, 1984).

According to the findings of the 1968 and 1973 Hacettepe University Surveys, adult women have very little say in decisions with respect to spending family income and choosing the friends or relatives to visit, although there is evidence of a slight improvement over time (Özbay, 1985, p. 71). In 1973, among various categories of decisions, the proportion of households in which decisions were jointly made by spouses ranged from a high of 26 per cent (in deciding which relatives to visit) to 17 per cent (in deciding how to spend family income) (Özbay, 1985, p. 72).

Despite the increasing availability of schools in rural areas, women's access to schooling is disproportionately low. Özbay (1985, p. 64) reports that according to the 1973 Hacettepe University Survey, 56 per cent of men and 31 per cent of women in rural areas had completed elementary school, and 13 per cent of men and 7 per cent of women a school beyond elementary education. Moreover, a comparative study of four Turkish villages shows that the educational attainment of women is inversely related to the agricultural workload they bear (Özbay, 1982).

Various folk sayings reflect the low social status of rural women and justify physical violence against women (Balaman, 1985), although the extent of physical abuse of women appears to vary by region and household economic standing (Özbay, 1982). Özbay observes that physical violence against women is common in households where women are in charge of agricultural production as well as in landless households in south-eastern Turkey, where both men and women are seasonal wage workers.

Research objectives and main hypotheses

This study will shed light on the directions and extent of change in the traditional patterns which circumscribe women's position in rural Turkish society as women engage in paid work. The primary objective is to produce information on conditions of women's work in carpet production in the context of both the organisation of carpet weaving and agrarian transformation in rural Turkey. The specific research objectives are as follows:

(a) to study the prevailing organisation of the carpet industry in rural areas and to evaluate the implications of different relations of production in weaving for women's productivity and earnings;

(b) to analyse the relationship between carpet weaving and other productive activities in rural areas in terms of the economic position of the weaving household, the role of weaving earnings, and demands on weavers' labour time;

(c) to measure the economic contribution of carpet weavers; and

(d) to evaluate the interaction of the weaver's economic role and her social position.

The main hypotheses are the following:

1. The participation of rural households in non-agricultural economic activities is generally attributed to the inability of these

5

households to support themselves on the basis of incomes from agricultural production due to insufficient landholdings (de Janvry, 1981; Dixon, 1981). We would therefore expect to find an inverse relationship between the magnitude of agricultural incomes and the volume of weaving. Alternatively, the agrarian structure could affect the volume of carpet weaving via women's work responsibilities in agriculture. Thus, the type of crops and the degree of mechanisation of crop production are expected to affect the weaving labour supply. Labour-intensive crops are likely to demand substantial time of women and limit the amount of time that they can devote to weaving.

2. A widely accepted argument in the feminist literature is that a sexual division of labour with women's primary responsibility for reproduction limits the kinds of paid work women are able to pursue and thereby constrains their ability to make important monetary contributions to their household (Benería, 1979; Barrett, 1980). (Reproductive responsibilities here refer to the bearing and rearing of children and the provision of daily services to meet the consumption needs of household members.) According to this argument, female carpet weavers with greater reproductive responsibilities would be forced to weave at home or would work intermittently in workshops, and in general these weavers would have a lower carpet output. The hypothesis that there exists a conflict between women's reproductive responsibilities and the extent and form of their weaving is based on the assumption that nuclear family organisation is prevalent and that other forms of assistance among women are absent. However, a particular household composition or the availability of extra-household assistance may alleviate the burden of some of the reproductive tasks, and hence women's reproductive work burden may not impede their ability to earn. If there are other women in the household, not only would the weaver's reproductive responsibilities be lessened, but household women might also specialise among various reproductive tasks. Therefore, combined with the fact that carpet weaving is usually a co-operative undertaking, the number of women in the household directly and indirectly determines the volume of weaving and household weaving income.

3. Workshop weaving results in greater output relative to home weaving, due to the uninterrupted full-time nature of the activity. The ability to maintain full-time weaving requires a higher degree of specialisation among women in the household. Therefore, workshop weaving is more feasible in regions where extended family organisation is prevalent. The division of labour in extended families will reflect women's position in the household hierarchy, where older women assume responsibility for domestic chores and maintain discipline over young women to ensure the latter's higher productivity in workshops.

4. Carpet weaving counters the proletarianisation or impoverishment of the rural household. The majority of households have access to land for subsistence, if not cash crop, agriculture. In addition, most households are independent producers in weaving. Even if the household does not have access to productive resources, weaving income is sufficient to reproduce the present economic position of the household given the continuing expansion of the market for carpets.

5. The feminist literature makes the hypothesis that participation in paid work affects women's position via the magnitude or relative importance of women's income. Two alternative hypotheses with respect to the relationship between women's income contribution and their position have been formulated:

(a) the greater the relative importance of the woman's income, the greater her autonomy is expected to be. It is argued that the magnitude of the woman's income and its share in total household income are the important determinants of female autonomy, when compared to simply having a paid job (Stoler, 1977; Roldán, 1985);

(b) the subordination of women is insensitive to, or even adversely affected by, the magnitude of female income or its proportion in household income. Some argue that the strength of the patriarchal ideology can prevent the translation of women's economic role into increased autonomy for women (Safilios-Rothschild, 1982). Others argue that the enhanced economic value of women's labour, in the context of traditional patriarchal social relations, may lead men to intensify their control over women (Elson and Pearson, 1981).

Research methodology

The study is based on a survey of carpet weavers in ten case study villages conducted between March and December 1983 in Turkey. The quantitative data reported in this monograph come from 133 structured interviews with carpet weavers. In addition, the study heavily relies upon information generated through participant observation, open-ended and group interviews with weavers, and open-ended interviews with merchants, workshop operators and exporters in the carpet trade, as well as with government and weaving co-operative officials.

The case study villages are located in the major weaving regions of Turkey (see figure 1). These villages were selected on the basis of two main criteria: representativeness in terms of relations of production in weaving in rural Turkey, and in terms of the agrarian structure at the regional level.[5] At the outset, it will be useful to summarise the characteristics of each village in terms of the history of weaving organisation and the agrarian structure. In the text, these villages are identified by the name of the nearest town or provincial centre.

Afyon (N=11):[6] Weaving was introduced in the late 1960s when the co-operative was established and Sümerbank - the state economic enterprise involved with textile production - provided weaving training. Weaving is carried out in homes using yarn and looms put out by Sümerbank. The cultivation of several labour-intensive cash crops (opium poppies, sugar beet, potatoes) creates opportunities for women to engage in wage work and the reciprocal exchange of labour for the major part of the year. The workload in agriculture, coupled with low piece-rates in the type of carpet produced for the low- and

8

Figure 1: Case study villages

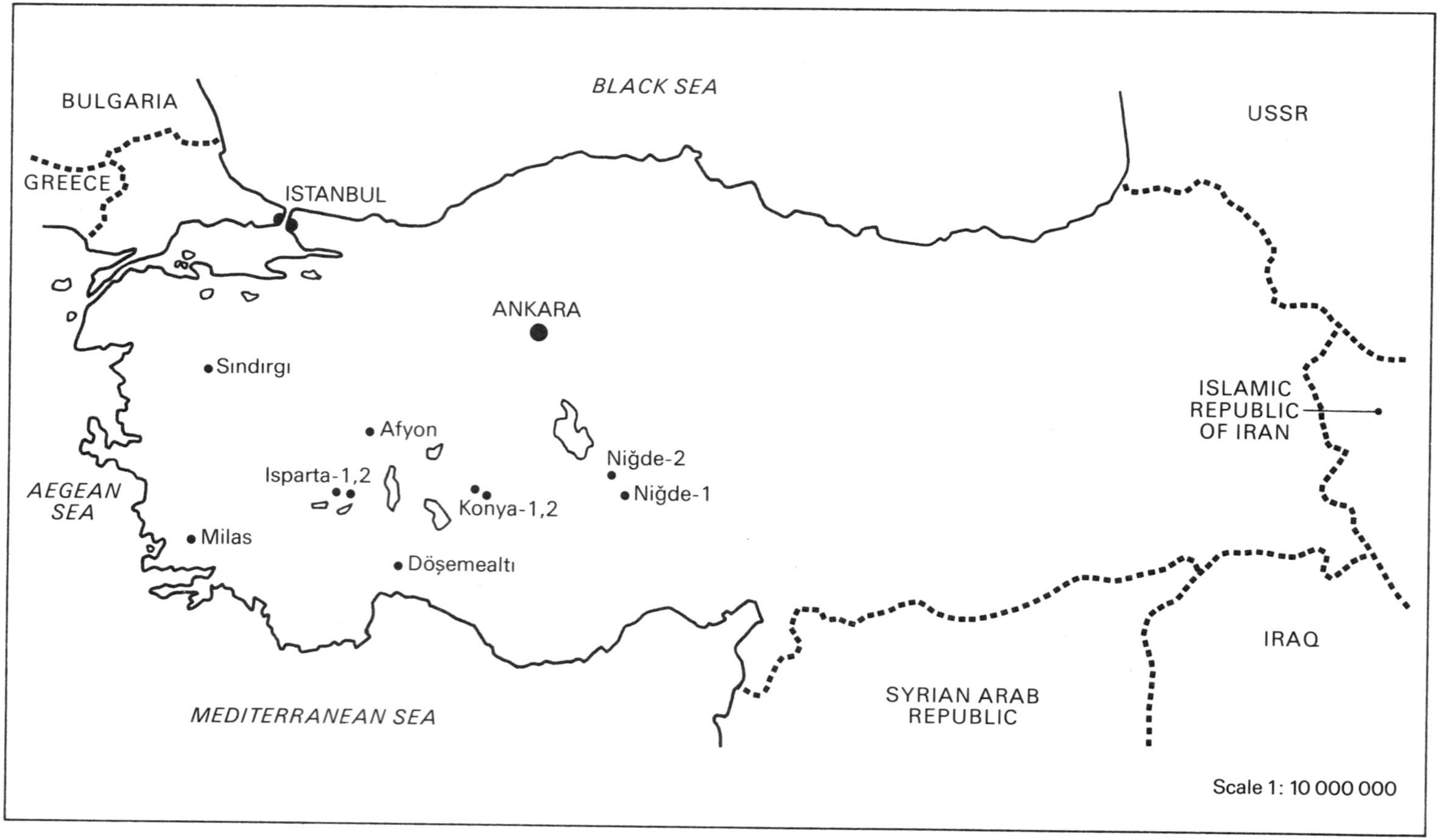

BULGARIA

GREECE

ISTANBUL

BLACK SEA

USSR

ANKARA

ISLAMIC
REPUBLIC
OF IRAN

●Sındırgı

Afyon
●

Isparta-1,2
●

Konya-1,2
●

Niğde-2
●

Niğde-1
●

●Milas

●Döşemealtı

AEGEAN
SEA

MEDITERRANEAN SEA

SYRIAN ARAB
REPUBLIC

IRAQ

Scale 1: 10 000 000

middle-income domestic market, renders weaving a marginal activity in this village. In the small proportion of village households in which weaving is undertaken, the activity is pursued in the winter months.

Niğde-1 (N=19): In this village of long-standing commodity production in weaving, carpets for the low-income domestic market are produced by independent producers. Recently, a new type of carpet for export is being introduced under the putting-out system in the village. Fruit production is the main cash crop in the village, and provides limited seasonal work for both men and women. A number of factories in the region also provide wage work for some men and women. For the majority of households weaving is a year-round activity.

Isparta-1, 2 (N=20): In these two neighbouring villages, weaving was introduced in the early 1950s by merchants from the provincial centre of Isparta. Production was initially geared to meet domestic demand. Until the mid-1970s the putting-out system and independent production co-existed in both villages, when merchants began putting out finer export carpets in response to the contraction of the domestic market for the particular carpet produced. This shift was accompanied by a move from independent production to the putting-out system and workshop production. Today the majority of weaving takes place in workshops controlled by intermediaries. Most households produce fruit and vegetables for weekly regional markets. Limited seasonal wage work in agriculture is available for both men and women. Weaving is a year-round activity in these villages, although attendance in work-shops and the rate of weaving drop during the summer months.

Konya-1, 2 (N=24): Weaving was introduced in the late 1950s in these two neighbouring villages under the putting-out system. A type of carpet geared to the domestic market was produced until the mid-1960s when the shift to finer export carpets took place. Today the majority of production takes place in workshops where intermediaries organise production on behalf of urban merchants and the village co-operative. In both villages, weaving is the principal source of income and is a year-round activity. Mechanised cereal cultivation is undertaken by share-cropper farmers, who take on the cultivation of small plots owned by other households. While wage work in agriculture is virtually non-existent, the mercury mine in the region provides stable employment for older men from about one-third of village house-holds.

Niğde-2 (N=15): A long-standing weaving tradition has been revived in the last two decades. Carpets are woven under independent production for the export market. Mechanised grain farming is carried out by a few share-cropper farmers on behalf of those with small landholdings, but most households are landless. Weaving is considered the principal source of household income and is a year-round activity in the village. In addition, some men work as self-employed or employed lorry drivers.

Milas (N=15): A long-standing weaving tradition has been revived and commodity production has expanded since the early 1960s. Production is mainly directed to the export market. The village is a smallholder village, where tobacco and olive oil production constitute the principal sources of income for most households. In most households weaving is carried out for about four months a year, between the olive harvest and tobacco cultivation and harvest seasons.

Döşemealtı (N=14): Weaving has spread in the last decade from a traditional weaving village in the region. Carpets are woven under independent production for the export market. All households have access to small plots, where they engage in year-round cultivation of fresh vegetables for regional markets as well as the nearby Antalya metropolitan market. In most households weaving is carried out for eight months a year.

Sındırgı (N=15): Weaving has spread in the last decade from a neighbouring village of traditional weaving. Carpets are turned out by independent producers and are destined for the export market. Most households engage in the production of tobacco as a cash crop. In most households weaving is pursued for up to six months a year.

*   *   *

The book is organised as follows: Chapter 1 reviews the policy debates and recommendations with respect to the carpet industry and summarises the changes in the structure of the industry since the early 1960s. Chapter 2 presents the demographic characteristics of a sample of weavers and their households, and describes work relations under differing relations of production. The main objective of this chapter is to show how relations of production in weaving and household composition interact to determine weaving output and earnings. Chapter 3 analyses the economic position of weaving households, discusses the effects of the agrarian structure on weaving output and explores the impact of the income contribution of weavers to the household's economic standing. Chapter 4 evaluates the impact of participation in a cash-generating activity on the weaver's position. It focuses on various aspects of women's position and explores the factors which account for variations in these dimensions across the sample. Finally, Chapter 5 summarises the main findings of the study and assesses the possibilities for improvement in the working conditions and the social position of rural carpet weavers.

Notes

[1] In what follows the terms "knotted carpets" and "handwoven carpets" are used interchangeably.

[2] The nature, sources and extent of underestimation of women's participation in productive work in the Third World are well documented in Benería (1982) and Deere and de Leal (1982).

[3] Ayata (1982) is the first systematic study that examines the organisation of the carpet industry in the Kayseri region, analysing the characteristics of the weaving labour force, aspects of production and retail marketing of carpets.

[4] For a recent attempt to synthesise research findings on rural women in Turkey see Kandiyoti (1984). The two main collections of essays on Turkish women are N. Abadan-Unat (ed.): Women in Turkish society (Leiden, Brill, 1981) and Çiğdem Kağıtçıbaşı (ed.): Sex roles, family and community in Turkey (Indiana, Indiana University Turkish Studies, 1982).

[5] The research methodology is described in Appendix I.

[6] The number of structured interviews with weavers in each village is indicated in parentheses.

CHAPTER 1

BACKGROUND TO THE CARPET INDUSTRY

This chapter first reviews the state policy vis-à-vis the carpet
industry in terms of exports, production and employment, focusing on
the 1960-80 period. Secondly, the evolution of the structure of
employment in response to the changing demand for carpets during this
period is discussed.

State policy

Carpet weaving received official recognition as a potential
source of foreign exchange earnings as well as rural incomes with the
First Five-Year Development Plan in 1963. An important source of
information on the state of the industry and policy considerations
during the plan period is the reports prepared by the advisory
committees on the carpet industry for each Five-Year Development Plan.
These committees are formed of government officials, carpet exporters
and merchants. The tenor of policy recommendations contained in the
Specialised Commission Reports (SCRs) reflects the heterogeneous
composition of the Commission and is generally geared towards development, if not representative of the views of major exporters and
merchants in the carpet trade.

Policy formulation has focused on export-promotion and production-
related measures, and not on conditions of employment. As regards the
production-related measures, the early SCRs focused on two objectives:
the expansion of handwoven carpet production and the improvement in
the quality of weaving. Increasing rural employment and expanding the
supply of high-quality carpets were expected to achieve the dual
goals of rural development and growth of foreign exchange reserves.

Early in the plan period, policy-makers recognised that fast
rates of urbanisation in Turkey and growth in GNP per head would
rapidly increase the demand for floor covering and lead to a deterioration in the quality of weaving and materials used, thus jeopardising
export growth. In order to meet growing demand with cheaper sub-
stitutes for handwoven carpets, policy-makers recommended subsidies
for machine-woven carpet production. The objective was to divide the
market into (a) low-income and (b) high-income and export groups, and
to preserve and improve the quality of handwoven carpets by meeting
the demands of these two segments by machine-woven and handwoven

carpets, respectively. Thus, machine-woven carpets were expected to alleviate demand pressure, which might have led to a deterioration in the quality of handwoven carpets.

The SCRs also recommended the formation of workshops and weaving co-operatives. Workshop weaving was expected to lead to a higher volume of production as well as improvements in the quality of carpets, presumably through direct control over designs, materials and weaving quality. The SCRs recognised the vast potential weaving labour force in Turkey and the regional disparities in its exploitation, and recommended integrated training-production schemes by the public sector to make use of the potential labour supply (DPT, 1966; DPT, 1972). In these schemes, the rural weaving co-operatives were expected to play an important role both in organising production and in centralising the savings of producers.

From early 1970s onwards machine-woven carpet production expanded, and from 1966 onwards, Sümerbank played an active role in expanding the production of handwoven carpets in rural areas. Its role was one of an institutional "putter-out". Sümerbank extended training services in regions where there was no weaving tradition, provided looms and put out yarn for weaving. The village co-operatives were integral to the functioning of Sümerbank in the training of weavers, and the production and marketing of carpets.

Despite the policy concerns regarding the organisation of producers into co-operatives, the momentum in setting up co-operatives subsided by the 1970s and workshop production organised under the auspices of co-operatives became a reality in only a few cases. Part of the problem was a gradual change in policy away from an emphasis on the formation of co-operatives. Another problem was that the efforts of Sümerbank and other state agencies in extending weaving training, setting up co-operatives and extending credit to them were often uncoordinated and isolated.

Sümerbank also became involved in subcontracting arrangements with co-operatives and merchants. Some co-operatives obtain their yarn from Sümerbank in return for a contract to supply the carpets, receiving from Sümerbank a sum based on a price per square meter, which includes labour costs and an intermediation fee to the co-operative. However, the largest proportion of carpets woven for Sümerbank are produced by merchants who receive yarn from Sümerbank, put out the weaving and turn in the carpets in return for a price per square meter. Since Sümerbank is slow to adjust the prices to market conditions, during periods of market expansion, co-operatives sell their carpets to merchants who offer higher prices. When the market is slack, however, the subcontracting arrangements of Sümerbank provide a guarantee which both the co-operatives and merchants rely upon. In turn, Sümerbank sells carpets in the domestic market through a chain of stores and exports a small number of silk carpets.

In policy formulation and recommendations, the weavers themselves and their working conditions receive limited attention. In general, the labour supply for weaving and the conditions of employment are assumed to be unproblematic. The widely held view among government officials and exporters alike is that carpet weaving is beneficial because it creates employment and enhances the earnings of rural households. It is claimed that through weaving an otherwise unemployed labour force is provided with work (Durusel, 1983), and thereby the population in these regions is transformed from consumers to producers (Özden, 1979, p. 86). Carpet weaving is hailed as the solution to the rural-urban migration problem by providing employment for peasants, who would otherwise migrate due to insufficient incomes from landholdings. In the same documents, however, the importance of the activity is played down. Weaving is regarded almost as "non-work", because it is done indoors and seated; it is seen as a "pastime" activity through which household incomes are supplemented (DPT, 1966; Durusel, 1983). Thus, the case for promotion of the industry is even further strengthened: weaving incomes increase and household living standards improve through this form of "non-work".

Only in the more recent SCRs are the working conditions recognised as unhealthy and appalling and the absence of any benefits for the weavers is explicitly stated (DPT, 1976; DPT, 1982; Celbiş, 1979). Under the Social Security Law (SSL), all workshop weavers are supposed to be covered by the social security system, which offers retirement and disability benefits as well as free health care in state health institutions. In practice, very few weavers, mostly in urban workshops, are covered by the SSL, and the invisibility of the rural workshop, coupled with legal loopholes, makes it very difficult to enforce compliance from employers.[1] The SSL imposes a 33.5 per cent contribution on the minimum wage, 19.5 per cent paid by the employer and 14 per cent by the weaver. According to employers, however, weavers or their families are unwilling to pay their contribution share, so that employers' compliance with the SSL can only materialise if employers pay both their own contribution and that of the workers. This, employers claim, renders workshop weaving too costly. In addition, they maintain that the seasonal nature of weaving and chronic absenteeism, and the piece-rate method of payment, create too much paperwork and make coverage very cumbersome. These factors open the way to the bribery of social security inspectors by employers to keep them away from workshops.

It is unfortunate that the law which is intended to safeguard the benefits of workshop weavers in effect prevents the improvement of their working conditions. The smaller and darker the workshop, the more difficult it is to detect from the outside by social security inspectors. Hence, the worse the working conditions, the easier it is for the employer to evade the payment of contributions. This does not imply that employers deliberately create a poor work environment, but simply that the employer's objective of keeping costs low also makes the workshop, and hence the weavers, invisible in the rural landscape.

In the SCRs, as well as in policy recommendations made by industry representatives, the SSL is regarded as the major obstacle to the development of workshop weaving, and planners and industry representatives have made various recommendations for its revision. The proposed alternatives range from the exemption of co-operative workers from social security contributions to making coverage optional for the workers, and from exempting carpet weaving from the coverage of the law altogether to the payment of the weavers' contributions by the State. The main argument used to support revisions in the SSL is that weavers give up weaving after marriage and childbirth and therefore do not complete the 20 years of contributions required for retirement (DPT, 1982). Hence, to enforce the SSL is claimed to be futile, since the contributions paid by employers and weavers are thus wasted, due to the early abandonment of weaving.

Despite pressure from the industry and repeated recommendations of the SCRs, no revisions in the SSL with respect to the carpet industry have been implemented. While the SSL is still in effect, workshop weavers are de facto outside the coverage of any social security scheme.

Changes in the market and the structure of the industry

Since the early 1960s there has been a steady increase in carpet production. Table 1 shows the expansion of production and exports in square meters in the 1960-82 period. While carpet export figures are available, given the predominantly home-based nature of the industry, the total volume of carpet output cannot be directly measured. Estimates of production reported in the SCRs are based on data compiled by various chambers of commerce in weaving centres, the directorates of weaving co-operatives in provinces and other regionally based institutions. The carpet production figures reported in table 1 are estimates based on (a) the level of annual yarn production and the volume of weaving this can sustain; and (b) the number of looms (i.e. the weaving capacity) in Turkey. In the latter method, the estimate takes into account regional differences in varying carpet knot densities as well as in loom-use capacity.

Table 1: Volume of production and exports of knotted carpets, 1960-82 (figures in 1,000 square metres)

Year	Carpet production	Carpet exports
1960	1 400	29
1965	1 871	55
1970	3 500	84
1975	4 003	139
1980	4 345	264
1982	4 555	471

Sources: DPT (1966, 1972, 1976, 1982).

In the absence of systematic surveys and inadequate census data, the SCRs estimate the total employment in carpet weaving in Turkey by two methods: the average number of weavers that work at a loom, and

the annual square meter output per weaver. In the first method, the
estimated total number of weavers is based on the number of looms in
a given year, assuming on average two or three weavers to a loom. In
the second method, total weaving employment is estimated on the basis
of the volume of output in a given year, assuming that a weaver weaves
16 square meters of average grade carpet per year. Employment estimates for 1958-81 are presented in table 2. These figures indicate
that during this period there has been nearly a four-fold increase in
employment in carpet weaving.

Table 2: Employment in knotted carpet production, 1958-81

Year	Number of weavers
1958	147 693
1965	160 000
1969	199 125
1970	224 937
1975	415 200
1978	525 000
1981	577 800

Note: Employment figures for 1965 are based on the assumption that
       on the average two weavers weave at one loom; for 1970, the
       figure is based on the assumption that each weaver weaves
       16 m^2 per year; for 1975 and 1981, it is assumed that three
       weavers weave at one loom.

Sources: Türkiye Ticaret Odaları, Sanayi Odaları ve Ticaret Borsaları
         Birliği (1959); DPT (1966, 1972, 1976, 1982); Celbiş (1979).

     According to an industry study of 1959 (Türkiye Ticaret Odaları,
Sanayi Odaları ve Ticaret Borsaları Birliği, 1959), between 1955 and
1958 female weavers constituted 98 per cent of all weavers. After
1959, the employment figures are no longer broken down by sex,
although in a number of SCRs references are made to the fact that
97-99 per cent of weavers are women. There are male weavers who
weave in workshops located in prisons. Nevertheless, since the number
of looms in prisons represent less than 1 per cent of the total, it
is possible to infer that carpet weavers in Turkey are overwhelmingly
women. Undoubtedly, male weavers outside the prison system are not
accounted for in this estimate. The consensus among merchants and
employers in the trade, however, is that male weavers are rare and
their weaving is occasional.
     The growth of weaving employment between 1958 and 1981 indicates
that overall employment has not been negatively affected by the
expansion of machine-woven carpet production in the latter half of

the period. However, it is most likely that machine-woven carpet
production has slowed down the growth of overall employment in handwoven carpets. The employment impact on a regional basis may have
been drastic; but in the absence of longitudinal surveys it is
impossible to assess the regional effects of the introduction of
machine-woven carpets.

The rise in knotted carpet exports in the 1963-82 period is
presented in table 3. The export growth is attributed to a number of
factors. From 1963 onwards, handwoven carpet exporters benefited
from tax credits granted to exporters of manufactured goods. The
10 per cent tax credit on exports was adjusted to between 10 and 30
per cent in 1970. From the late 1970s onwards, the problems faced by
major carpet-exporting countries, the Islamic Republic of Iran and
Afghanistan, proved favourable to Turkey's exports of finer grades of
carpets. After 1980, aggressive export promotion policies adopted
under the military regime were a further boost to export growth. The
last two factors account for the steep rise in carpet exports between
1979 and 1982. While the absolute volume of exports has grown several-
fold, the share of knotted carpets in total exports has grown from
0.2 per cent to 3.8 per cent. The significance of the industry is
only partly captured by export statistics. A comparison of the volume
of production and exports in table 1 indicates that, despite the export
growth in recent years, exports still constitute only about 10
per cent of total carpet production in Turkey.

Table 3: Knotted carpet exports, manufacturing exports and total
exports, 1963-82
(figures in US$1,000)

Year	Knotted carpet exports	Manufactur- ing exports	Total exports	Share of knotted carpets in manufactur- ing exports (%)	Share of knotted carpets in total exports (%)
1963	1 074	9 968	368 087	11.0	0.2
1965	1 993	24 326	458 922	6.0	0.3
1970	2 622	43 236	588 523	6.1	0.5
1975	17 028	193 682	1 401 074	8.8	1.2
1980	81 129	490 901	2 909 635	16.5	2.8
1982	217 738	1 569 851	5 747 449	13.9	3.8

Sources: United Nations: Yearbooks of International Trade Statistics;
DPT (1972).

Capitalist development and the growth of both domestic and export
demand for handwoven carpets during the period 1963-82 have brought
about a number of important changes in the structure of employment.

While in 1960 commercial weaving was largely undertaken under the putting-out system, in the late 1970s the majority of weavers were estimated to be independent producers. Table 4 shows the structure of employment in 1958, 1965 and 1978. In 1958, merchant-controlled production (the putting-out system and workshop production) accounted for over three-quarters of total production, although only slightly over half of the total number of looms were controlled by merchants. Most of the weavers in this group wove under the putting-out system whereby the merchant provides the yarn and the loom. The independent weavers who wove carpets on their own account either could secure wool from their sheep or had the means to purchase yarn to weave one carpet at a time. The 1978 figures on shares of loom capacity indicate that two-thirds of the looms were controlled by independent producers. As the 1958 and 1965 figures indicate that the percentage of looms con-trolled tends to be an inaccurate indicator of the share of volume of production, the dramatic increase in the loom share of independent producers does not necessarily imply a commensurate increase in the share of independent production. Nevertheless, there is widespread agreement among merchants and exporters today that independent pro-ducers account for a larger share of employment, although both indepen-dent production and merchant-controlled production, particularly work-shop production, have expanded in recent years.

Table 4: The structure of the carpet industry (percentages)

Type of production	1958		1965		1978
	Looms	Square metres	Looms	Square metres	Looms/square metres
Merchant-controlled production	52.3	76.6	57.6	75.3	24.98
Independent household production	47.7	23.4	42.0	24.7	67.47
State-controlled production	*	*	*	*	1.95
Weaving co-operatives	*	*	*	*	5.60
Unused looms	*	*	0.4	*	*
Total	100.0	100.0	100.0	100.0	100.0

* = not available.

Note: This table should be interpreted with caution. As can be seen from the 1958 and 1965 figures, the percentage of looms con-trolled is not an accurate indicator of volume of production because looms controlled by independent household producers tend to be underused. The 1978 figures for shares in volume of pro-duction, however, are based on the assumption that the loom share is an accurate indicator of output share. If 1978 output figures had been measured independently of the number of looms, merchant-controlled weaving would have accounted for a larger, and independent household production a smaller, share than their reported shares of looms.

Sources: Türkiye Ticaret Odaları, Sanayi Odaları ve Ticaret Borsaları Birliği (1959); DPT (1966); Celbiş (1979).

The single most important reason underlying the co-existence and flourishing of both merchant-controlled and independent production in the face of growing demand, however, is that a known handicraft technique and simple means of production lie at the foundation of the production process. The production of a knotted carpet consists of a number of processes: shearing wool from sheep; combing and washing wool; spinning; making skeins of yarn; dyeing; making yarn balls; setting up the warp; and finally weaving. Today factory-spun and dyed yarn is used in most carpets produced in Turkey.[2] While some independent weavers undertake ancillary tasks related to weaving, under the putting-out system and especially in workshop production weavers are only concerned with the weaving itself.

The weaving stage involves tying individual knots to the vertical yarn strings (the warp) stretched on an upright wooden loom. The knots are tied in accordance with a pattern. After each row of knotting is completed, the weaver weaves one or two yarn threads (the weft) through the vertical yarn strings, and pounding on the weft yarn with a heavy comb she presses down the knotted row. The yarn ends of the knotted row (which altogether make up the pile of the carpet) are then cut to an even length with a pair of scissors and the weaver goes on to the knotting of the next row. Thus, depending on its size and the density of knots, a carpet consists of thousands, sometimes millions of knots. Weaving is carried out by one or more weavers depending on the width of the carpet. There is no technical division of labour in weaving, only simple co-operation of weavers who sit side by side at the loom. The technique is the same under all three relations of production.

The unmechanised, labour-intensive production process has implications for the social organisation of production and technical change. On the one hand, the weaving process is suitable for a variety of unit sizes from large workshops to domestic premises. On the other hand, the handicraft nature of the product rules out technical change from being introduced in the weaving stage. Since it is precisely the "handmade" quality of the product that underlies the strength of demand, hand-knotted carpets - unlike most non-agricultural products - are not likely to be displaced by their machine-woven counterparts in the course of capitalist development. As a result, not only do three relations of production (i.e. independent production, the putting-out system and workshop production) based on home and workshop labour processes[3] coexist, but it is also virtually impossible for merchants to monopolise the production technique and thereby expand their control over production.

Despite the absence of technical barriers for independent production to grow, the market is nevertheless segmented and, as indicated in table 5, independent producers tend to specialise in lower knot density and smaller carpets.[4] The independent producers are unwilling or unable to engage in the production of higher knot density and larger carpets, because these require a larger capital outlay and take longer to complete.

Besides the labour-intensive production technique, the changes in the relations of production in weaving are the outcome of a number

of influences discussed earlier. The increase in machine-woven
carpet production and the growth of incomes in the economy, as well
as the expansion of export markets and the development of rural transport networks, have set off tendencies for change in both directions.

Table 5: Average knot density of carpets by relation of production

	Average knot density[a]	N
Independent production	722	77
Putting-out system	994	17
Workshop production	1 749	39
Total		133

[a] Number of knots per 100 cm^2 of carpet.

Source: Survey of rural carpet weavers in Turkey, 1983. This survey
is the source of all subsequent tables in this study.

From the late 1960s onwards, along with the growth in high-
income domestic and export markets, a transformation occurred in the
nature of the product: a general upgrading of quality and a shift
towards weaving higher knot density carpets. While this has exerted
pressures for a transformation from independent production to merchant-
controlled weaving (the putting-out system and workshop production),
some low knot density regional carpets that came to be exported have
become the stronghold of independent production.

Machine-woven carpet production seems to have had the foreseen
impact of meeting part of the growing domestic demand for floor
covering (Ülker, 1979). The expansion of machine-woven carpet production represented competition with the low knot density and poor-
quality carpets. In regions where, prior to the expansion of machine-
woven production, these carpets were being produced under merchant
control, the merchants have switched to the weaving of finer carpet
groups. Where they were produced by independent producers, the
weavers have shifted to producing finer grades under the control of
merchants. Hence, the shrinking domestic demand in lower knot
density and inferior-quality carpets has set off a tendency for the
expansion of merchant-controlled weaving. Since finer wool carpets
also tend to be of larger sizes, the switch to finer grades has also
been accompanied by an increase in rural workshops, where larger looms
are set up and a greater number of weavers work on each loom. Thus,
while the introduction of machine-woven carpets does not seem to have
had a negative impact on overall employment in handwoven carpets, it has
reinforced the tendency towards a shift from independent production to
merchant-controlled weaving, in particular to production in workshops.

The expansion of workshop production has occurred in spite of
the alleged obstacle of social security contributions. The

contribution scale stipulated by the law has pushed production away from large centres and has counteracted the establishment of large workshops, but it has not inhibited rural workshop production. Social security contributions are seen by merchants as a source of unfair competition between themselves and independent producers, who weave using family labour and are therefore exempt. Yet, given that independent producers and workshop weavers weave different grades of carpets, there is no real competition. To the extent that the levying of contributions has been effective in the movement of workshop production towards more remote rural areas, however, it has forced merchants to rely on intermediaries and has led to the development of the subcontracting system.

The development of the rural transport network has both extended the putting-out system and strengthened independent production. Road construction has linked remote villages to markets as well as making sources of potential carpet weavers accessible to merchants. Finally, the growth of the cash nexus has probably made possible the growth of independent production.

Conclusion

In the post-1960 period, both the production of handwoven carpets and employment have greatly increased. This has been partly due to government efforts to extend weaving training and to organise co-operatives. Given the labour-intensive nature of the production process and the segmented market for carpets, the growth of demand for carpets in this period has brought about an expansion in both independent household production and merchant-controlled weaving. Much of the policy discussion centres on the product and not the producer. Weaving is not regulated by any special legislation, conditions of employment are generally viewed as unproblematic, and weavers remain invisible to policy-makers.

Notes

[1] For example, if weavers of a workshop are relatives living together, then the workshop is exempt from the tax.

[2] The use of chemical dyes and mechanisation of the yarn-spinning phase began in the mid-nineteenth century and at the turn of the century, respectively (Quataert, 1986). Today in some regions, for handspun quality yarn carpets, the spinning phase is still unmechanised.

[3] In this study, "labour process" refers to the social organisation of production, which encompasses work organisation and location and production technique.

[4] The knot density of a carpet, which refers to the number of knots per 10 cm^2, was measured during fieldwork.

22

CHAPTER 2

CHARACTERISTICS OF CARPET WEAVING EMPLOYMENT

This chapter examines various characteristics of rural carpet weaving. First, the demographic characteristics of weavers and the process of acquisition of weaving skills are presented. Secondly, the features of the three relations of production under which carpets are produced in Turkey today are discussed. A basic argument of this study is that relations of production have implications for both weaving earnings and the effects of participation in paid work on women's position. Hence, two dimensions of differing relations of production are examined: the relations between the weaver and the employer in terms of their respective control over means of production; and the quality of the work environment and the implications of sex and age for work relations. Following an examination of the factors that shape unit earnings, the effects of the weaving labour process and women's reproductive responsibilities in determining the weaver's volume of weaving are analysed. Finally, the work histories of weavers are evaluated.

Weavers: A demographic profile

Weavers are women of all ages, although 70 per cent of the 133 sample weavers are 30 years and younger,[1] with 39 per cent of weavers between the ages of 15 and 20. Workshop weavers are on average younger than home weavers. The mean age of weavers varies substantially across the case study villages, ranging from 19.5 in Afyon to 36.2 years in Niğde-1. Forty-one per cent of weavers are single and 53 per cent are married.

While 27.1 per cent of the sample weavers are illiterate, 63.2 per cent have completed the compulsory elementary schooling of five years. Only 4.5 per cent, all of whom are in the 15 to 20 age group, have had schooling beyond five years. Younger weavers are more likely to have completed elementary school than their older counterparts. Seventy-five per cent of weavers under the age of 31 as opposed to 35 per cent of those 31 years and older have completed elementary school.

The number of persons per household ranges from 1 to 10, with an average of 5.2 persons.[2] Fifteen per cent of sample weavers belong to households that are headed by a woman, where either the

weaver or her mother is the household head. In this study, female-
headed households were identified according to two criteria: (a) the
absence of the principal weaver's father or husband from the household
for more than six months a year; or (b) the permanent absence of the
adult male from the household. The first criterion captures the
de facto female-headed households resulting from the seasonal or
recurrent migration of men, while the second measures the incidence of
de jure female-headed households in which headship is assumed by
widowed or divorced women. These criteria therefore exclude nuclear
families that are part of an extended family residence, even if the
adult male of the nuclear family may be a migrant. They also exclude
families of young divorced or widowed weavers that live with their
natal families.

     In rural Turkey, patrilocality and patrilineality are the norm.
Marriage of sons usually brings about the formation of an extended
family household. However, in most case study villages, within a
few years after marriage these households break up into nuclear households. Fourteen per cent of sample households belong to extended
family households composed of a stem couple, their son(s), unmarried
daughter(s), daughter(s)-in-law and grandchildren. Some of these
households also include a widowed parent of the man of the stem
couple.[3]

     Extended family households in the sample are not necessarily asso-
ciated with larger landholdings, contrary to what is argued in various
studies (Timur, 1981; Kandiyoti, 1984). In a small proportion of
extended family households the economic basis of extendedness appears
to be the control of larger landholdings by the oldest male in the
household. Yet a greater number of extended family households
include wives and children of migrant sons, and the breakup of the
household into nuclear households is postponed by the seasonal,
recurrent or permanent migration pattern of sons. These are households with smaller landholdings, and the economic basis of the household organisation appears to be the pooling of resources to ensure
household subsistence.

The acquisition of weaving skills

     Weaving skills, which are the minimum skills possessed by all
weavers, are acquired through informal "on-the-job" training. All
but three weavers have learnt weaving from either a member of their
household (59 per cent), a relative or neighbour in their community,
and three-quarters have picked up weaving skills in a home setting.
Under the supervision of her experienced relative or neighbour, the
trainee weaves a small portion of each row until her speed reaches a
level which allows the number of knots in each row of the carpet to
be equally split among weavers at a loom.

     Weavers start contributing to weaving earnings when they begin
tying knots, even though it may take years to acquire all the
weaving skills described in Chapter 1 and reach a weaving speed
customary in the village. Knotting skills are acquired in the least

amount of time, while following a pattern, hitting the comb at an even force on a given row and across rows, and being able to shear the pile at an even thickness take considerably longer. Finally, picking up speed, and being able to co-ordinate the completion of each row of knots with co-weavers can take one to two years.

Given the lengthy process of the development of weaving skills, the labour involved can be classified as skilled labour, although neither the weavers nor their male kin consider it as such. Incompetence in any of the weaving skills is reflected in the carpet and diminishes its sale value. Uneven force with which the knotted row is hit with the comb results in waviness along the sides of the carpet when it is laid flat on the floor. Inability to follow the pattern and unevenness of pounding also result in distortions in the designs. Incompetence in shearing the pile at even thickness results in a fuzzy look of the pile, although it is possible for the retail merchant to correct this defect through industrial shearing.

Usually the training period is spread over a number of years of childhood. The general pattern is that weavers learn to knot between the ages of 6 and 10, start weaving at 12 and by the age of 13 or 14 are capable of weaving on their own. The median age at which sample weavers began weaving more or less continuously (i.e. they were no longer considered occasional knotters), is 12.2 years. It is important to note, however, that almost one-quarter of the weavers began weaving before the age of 11 and 93 per cent began before the age of 21. It seems that the ability to sit motionless at the loom for lengthy hours, with only the hands tying knots, can best be instilled in childhood.

Only in villages where weaving was recently introduced did women begin weaving in adulthood. In these villages, partly due to the fact that women did not have the "opportunity" to learn weaving at an earlier age, the average starting age is higher (17.7 years) relative to that in traditional weaving villages (11.8 years). In villages of traditional weaving, older weavers started weaving at an earlier age than their younger counterparts, while in villages where weaving is a recent development, younger weavers begin weaving at an earlier age than older weavers. In both village groups, compared to older weavers younger weavers are more likely to have begun weaving after completing elementary school. This is largely due to the changing attitudes towards the education of girls, the increasing availability of elementary schools in the case study villages and the overall improvement in the economic position of rural households over time.

To sum up, the weaving labour force is trained at no cost to merchants and employers. Even in workshops, merchants do not formally arrange the training of new weavers. Since each trainee is under the supervision of the relative with whom she weaves side by side, the likelihood of errors being made by the trainee is quite low. In effect, the employer has one instructor per trainee. Merchants prefer putting out carpets in locations where weaving skills already exist. The village could be one in which carpets have been woven tradition- ally, even if presently only a few women possess weaving skills. In these villages, as merchant-controlled weaving takes hold, skills are rapidly transmitted to women of all ages. The village could also be one where Sümerbank or some other state institution has recently provided weaving training and set up a weaving co-operative.

Relations of production in carpet weaving

The retail merchant or exporter in large urban areas is linked to the actual weaver through layers of intermediaries. It is rare for exporters to be directly involved in organising production. Their involvement is limited to arrangements with regional merchants, who arrange weaving under the putting-out system, either directly or by subcontracting to intermediaries, and buy carpets from dealers, who in turn collect carpets from independent weavers. As the following discussion will show, the weaver's relationship to the last link in this chain is often not direct but through her male kin. In most cases, carpets or the woman's labour power are sold by her husband, father or brother. Thus, in what follows, references to the weaver or the household as an agent should be taken to imply the intermediation of men and limited decision-making power and control by the individual female weaver.

Weavers and their families have little choice over the relation of production under which they are to produce carpets. The carpet historically produced in the village or region, or recently introduced by merchants or some state institution, limits their choice. As will be discussed below, the relation of production under which carpets are woven, however, largely determines the magnitude of weaving income, via the piece-rate and the rate of weaving engendered by the weaving labour process.

Over half the sample weavers are independent producers, while 29 per cent weave in a workshop and 13 per cent weave under the putting-out system. When grouped by labour process, the sample consists of 39 workshop weavers and 94 home-based weavers. An institutional breakdown reveals that 27 weavers weave for a weaving co-operative, while 29 weave for a merchant or intermediary and 77 are independent weavers (table 6).

All workshop weavers and the majority of home weavers weave with at least one other weaver. Only about 15 per cent of home weavers in this study weave carpets alone. Whether they weave at home or in a workshop, the norm among sample weavers is to weave together with household members. In 56.4 per cent of sample households there are at least two weavers. Yet over half the sample weavers co-operate with at least one non-household weaver.

Independent production

Under independent production weaving is done in the living quarters of the home, using the loom, yarn, comb and pair of scissors owned by the household. Independent weavers exercise control over

Table 6: Distribution of sample weavers by employer

	N	%
Merchant	9	6.8
Intermediary to merchant	20	15.0
Independent production: only for market	67	50.4
Independent production: for market and specific customer	10	7.5
Weaving co-operative	11	8.3
Intermediary to weaving co-operative	16	12.0
Total	133	100.0

the production process by allocating their time to weaving and non-weaving tasks. Upon completion, the carpet is sold on the market. Thus, independent weavers, or more accurately the male heads of independent producer households, have control over the product.

As stated earlier, independent production is predominant in smaller or lower knot density carpets (see table 5). In addition, a large proportion of independent weavers in this study weave the so-called Anatolian carpets, characterised by the use of hand-spun yarn dyed with vegetable dyestuffs, and traditionally produced in certain regions for use. Economic rather than technical considerations discussed in Chapter 1 circumscribe the possibilities for weaving under independent production. Higher knot density and larger carpets take longer to complete, and hence independent weaving households are usually unable or reluctant to tie up resources in lengthy production. Even if they were able to finance the production of finer carpets and had a sufficient number of household weavers, the uncertainty surrounding the marketing of the high-cost item would deter them from weaving higher knot density and larger carpets. The main determinant of market-oriented weaving in the form of independent production is the ease with which carpets can be marketed, yarn obtained and costs recouped by the weaving household.

Independent producers, unlike the workshop and putting-out system weavers, undertake some ancillary tasks in carpet production. While the range of tasks performed by household members varies regionally and by type of carpet, these tasks are overwhelmingly undertaken by female household members. In some regions dyed yard is readily purchased, while in others weavers are involved in combing wool, spinning yarn and dyeing the yarn with natural or commercial dyes. However, in very few independent households are all the stages of carpet production undertaken. Table 7 shows the extent to which weaving-related tasks are carried out by members of independent households and the incidence of male participation in these tasks. Setting up the warp strings is a task carried out in almost all independent households, with a few households relying on a neighbour for the task, and in most yarn is washed and some colours dyed.

In households where yarn is spun, wool is obtained from family-owned sheep or bought on the market. Wool is usually washed at public taps prior to spinning. Yarn is spun for any one or a combination of the various types of yarn requirements of the carpet: the warp, the knotting yarn and the weft. This task is undertaken in few households, and in none of them do men engage in spinning.

Table 7: Distribution of weaving-related tasks and participation of men in these tasks in independent weaving households[a]

	No. of households in which task is undertaken (1)	No. of households in which men participate[b] (2)	% of men participating (2)/(1)
Spinning wool	20	0	0
Dyeing yarn	68	5	7
Washing wool	14	1	7
Washing yarn	52	6	12
Making skeins	67	7	10
Making balls	77	16	21
Setting up warp	73	16	22

[a] The total number of independent weaving households is 77.

[b] Except in setting up warp, in each household there is only one male household member that participates in each task.

After the yarn is spun and made into balls, skeins of yarn are made to allow better dye absorption. If factory-spun yarn is used, it must often be washed with detergent in boiling water prior to dyeing to get rid of the excess grease added during factory spinning. Yarn is dyed by boiling dyestuffs, either natural or synthetic, together with the yarn in a cauldron. Depending on the number of colours in the carpet and the extent of preparation of dyestuffs, dyeing can take up to several days. Usually yarn for a number of carpets is dyed all together. After dyeing, the yarn is taken to public taps and thoroughly rinsed. Even if they use factory-spun yarn in weaving, most independent weavers dye at least some colours themselves.

Finally, at least two people in addition to the experienced "warper" are needed in order to set up the warp. Where female household members are insufficient in number, the assistance of the male members or neighbours is obtained. Among the weaving-related tasks,

this is the task in which the participation of men is the highest.
Men are involved in setting up the warp in 22 per cent of households
in which this task is undertaken (table 7).

As noted earlier, weaving is a co-operative undertaking.
Depending on the size of the carpet, two or three weavers co-operate
in weaving. In 18 per cent of independent households there is a male
member who weaves along with the principal weaver, but only 9 per cent
have a man who is a frequent weaver. All independent households who
have a male weaver are located in the Milas and Sındırgı villages.
Whether or not men engage in weaving can be attributed to a number of
factors. First, the relatively flexible sexual division of labour in
tobacco farming probably makes it easier for men in these villages to
accept sharing weaving work with women. Second, in most of these
households there appears to be a shortage of women. Moreover, since
most of these households do not have either a sufficient number of
family members or access to land to engage in labour-intensive
tobacco farming, they rely heavily on carpet weaving to ensure household subsistence.

To make up for the shortage of household weavers and to complete
carpets in reasonable time, independent weavers engage in exchange of
labour with neighbours and kin. This involves the co-operation of
weavers from two households in the production of carpets for each
household. Accordingly, members of each household prepare the yarn
to be used in the weaving of their own carpet and the weaving is
undertaken by weavers from both households. After the completion of
the carpet for one household, the weaver from the first household
reciprocates and works at the loom of the second household with the
weaver or weavers of the second household in the production of a
carpet for them. Alternatively, the system can be based on exchanging
a certain number of weaving days and does not necessarily involve the
exchange of the total period required for the completion of a carpet
for each household.

Thirty-five per cent of the independent weavers in the sample
exchange their labour. Through this informal network the pace of
weaving can be kept up, not only because of simple co-operation, but
also because the exchange of labour alleviates the isolation and
boredom of the home weaver. Moreover, interruptions are minimised
and, except for lunch breaks, the continuity of weaving is kept up.
Weavers who exchange their labour usually do not have young children,
because children cause interruptions and slow down the pace of
weaving, which the weaving partner may not tolerate.

When the weaving is completed, the carpet is sold to a dealer,
either in the village or at the weekly market in the nearby town.
Slightly over one-half (54.8 per cent) of independent weavers sell
carpets in their homes to local dealers. In 68.5 per cent of the
households, carpets are sold by a male relative of the principal
weaver. In only 23.3 per cent of independent households are women
involved in the sale of the carpets they have produced, and this
practice is concentrated in the Niğde-1 case study village.

In the case study villages, carpets can be sold with relative
ease. In 70 per cent of independent households, carpets are sold

immediately after the completion of weaving. Seventy-seven per cent of weavers gave "the need for income" as their reason for the immediate sale. Those who did not sell immediately regard carpets as "savings" and claim to have no urgent need to sell.

Earnings under independent production are based on a payment per square meter or per carpet. Unless the sale is made to a local dealer or to a yarn merchant, the sum is paid in full at the time of the sale. Sixty-five per cent of the independent weavers who sold carpets in 1983 were paid the full sum at the time of the sale.

To characterise independent household production as "independent" is slightly inaccurate. Most independent households are dependent on yarn dealers. Given their limited resources, the poorer peasants usually purchase yarn on credit at a higher price, and the merchant who sells the yarn often is the same person as the buyer of the carpet. Moreover, the fact that carpets are mostly collected by village dealers enhances the bargaining power of dealers. Knowledge of the financial position of the household makes it possible for the dealer to bargain for the lowest possible price for the carpet. Finally, village dealers transmit information on the most desired designs to weavers, and sometimes even introduce the weaving of a totally new type of carpet by bringing a sample carpet from the export or retail merchant. Thus, although the export or retail merchant seems removed from actual production, through village dealers he exerts considerable control over carpet prices as well as over the volume of production in the desired patterns.

While the majority of independent weavers produce carpets exclusively for the market, a small percentage (most of them in the Döşemealtı village) also weave carpets to order for specific customers from the village who provide the yarn to the weaver (see table 6). Weaving to order is a limited practice among sample weavers, yet it seems to have been common in other regions as well prior to the wide-spread availability of machine-spun yarn. Earlier, families that did not own sheep, could not afford yarn, or were unable to market the carpet, wove carpets for households without any weavers. While the order carpets were originally produced for personal use, in recent years some of the customers started acting as intermediaries to urban merchants. The practice seems to be disappearing altogether, however, along with the increased marketing opportunities for carpets and the widespread availability of factory-spun yarn.

Before concluding the discussion of independent production, it is important to point out the quality of work relations in independent production. Engaging in weaving as an income-generating activity does not bring independent weavers into contact with any strangers, but represents a continuity of social relations of which weavers are already a part. They weave at home with their sisters, mothers and daughters. If they engage in reciprocal labour exchange, they come into contact with more distant relatives or neighbours. Their fathers and husbands or senior women in the household act as intermediaries in selling the carpets they produce.

The putting-out system

The primary difference between the putting-out system and
independent production is the lack of control of the actual producers
over the product in the former, while both groups of weavers exercise
control over the production process. The merchant or his employees
provide the yarn, designs, and sometimes also the looms to the
weavers. The employee periodically visits the weavers' homes, sets
up the warp, collects the finished carpets and pays out wages based
on a piece-rate per 1,000 knots. In Konya and Isparta regions,
where inter-merchant competition is intense, a new practice is to pay
a fee per carpet to the putting-out system weavers (hereafter referred
to as outworkers) in addition to their wages. This fee is intended to
make the weaving of larger carpets attractive to weavers, to speed up
their weaving, and to guarantee their "loyalty".
If the merchant is not located close to the production region,
he relegates the responsibility of distributing the means of production
and collecting the carpets to a single intermediary in the village,
who often is a wealthy peasant and whose female kin oversee the
distribution of yarn and supervise the weaving. The intermediary
in turn receives a supervision fee over and above the weavers' wages
paid by the merchant.
The putting-out system does not appear to be closely identified
with a particular type of carpet. Over half the outworkers in this
study produce lower knot density carpets that are sold in the low-
income domestic market. These are weavers of the Afyon village to
whom Sümerbank provides the looms, designs and yarn, and pays wages
through the village co-operative that acts as a non-profit intermediary. The piece-rates are set and periodically adjusted by
Sümerbank and neither the co-operative nor the weavers have any
bargaining power in wage determination. The Sümerbank piece-rates
usually serve as a minimum rate below which piece-rates offered
by merchants in the area in question do not fall.
The rest of the outworkers weave higher knot density export
carpets, and most of them are located in Konya and Isparta villages
where production in workshops is predominant. Some weavers weave at
home because their child-care responsibilities do not allow them to
weave in workshops. Others take advantage of the per carpet bonus,
if there is a sufficient number of women at home to allow the full-
time commitment to the weaving of a large carpet without hindering
the performance of daily domestic responsibilities.
As with independent weavers, the putting-out system does not
introduce outworkers to a new set of social relations. Under neither
putting-out system nor independent production do women own or possess
the means of production in their own right. Outworkers remain within
the confines of their home and have no contact with persons who are
not household members, except for the periodic short visits of the
intermediary with whom the oldest woman in the household deals.

Workshop production

Workshop production can be distinguished from the putting-out system by the producer's lack of control over the production process in the former, by virtue of the fact that weaving is organised in a workplace outside the home. Workshop weavers (or the male head of their household) do not own or possess the means of production. Weavers have no skills pertaining to carpet production but weaving skills. In workshop production, the merchant supplies the yarn, designs, and frequently also the looms, to an intermediary who owns and operates a workshop. The rural workshop is a room of two to five looms where between eight and 30 weavers weave. It is usually located in or attached to the home of the intermediary. The intermediary employs the weavers, who are his relatives or neighbours, and pays them wages, which are reimbursed by the merchant in advance or upon completion of the carpet. The workshop operator is often a prosperous peasant who is able to finance wage payments and advances to weavers, until he is reimbursed by the merchant. In return for each square metre of carpet the intermediary turns in to the merchant, he receives a fee. The Konya village co-operatives also act as merchants, providing means of production to intermediaries, and in turn selling carpets to urban merchants and exporters. In this instance, it is the co-operative which extends the weavers' wages and pays the fee per square metre to the workshop operator.

In rural workshops there is no direct supervision of working hours or quality of weaving by the intermediary. None the less, as will be discussed below, regular working hours are institutionalised in both regions of workshop weaving and make possible a greater rate of weaving. Because of this, and the fact that this labour process enables large carpets to be produced as well as enhancing control over the product (to the extent that the scatter of weavers is reduced), the merchant who provides the production materials to the workshop operators favours workshop weaving over home weaving. The risk involved in workshop production emanates from the fact that working conditions in workshops border on illegality. The major threat is the SSL, although evasion of contributions and controls is widespread. At the first sight of an inspector in the village, it is alleged, weavers are rapidly dispersed, or they are instructed to say that they are all relatives or that the carpets they weave are for their personal use.

Like the outworkers, workshop weavers are paid on the basis of a piece-rate per 1,000 knots. Wages are paid either upon completion of the carpet or on a weekly basis. In the former method, earnings per carpet, calculated on the basis of the piece-rate and the number of knots in the carpet, are divided by the number of weavers at the loom. In the weekly payment method, earnings are based on a daily accounting of the volume of weaving. In the Konya case study villages, a system of advances on wages is a widespread method of control over labour by merchants. The intermediaries extend wage advances to the male kin of the weaver and thereby tie up the worker for periods of time. Consequently, weavers at a loom are often indebted to the intermediaries.

As soon as the debt is paid through weaving, the weaver's male relative tries to get a second advance.

Finally, as regards social relations, the introduction of wage labour in workshops does not represent a new mode of interaction either among weavers or between the weaver and her employer. Her employer as well as her fellow workers are her relatives, or at most co-residents of the same village community. The personal relationships embodying gender and age hierarchies are recreated in the workplace. There are differences, however, in the quality of social relations in workshops between the two regions of workshop weaving. As explained below, social relations in Konya workshops appear to be more hierarchical than those in Isparta workshops. The difference seems to result from a wider age range of Konya weavers. Relations in Konya workshops are also more exclusively based on kinship ties.

Weaving earnings

This section explores the factors which shape the principal weavers' incomes under the three relations of production discussed above. Table 8 reveals that on average daily and annual incomes are highest for workshop weavers and lowest for outworkers.[4] It may be seen that lower output accounts for the low relative annual and daily earnings of independent producers, even though their unit earnings (earnings per 1,000 knots) are on average substantially higher than those of the outworkers and workshop weavers. Similarly, due to the combination of low output and lowest piece-rates, the outworkers earn the lowest annual and daily earnings among weavers.

Table 9 shows average daily and unit earnings by village, as compared with daily wages in seasonal agricultural work. On average, daily earnings are highest in the Konya villages and lowest in the Niǧde-1 village. The second and third columns of table 9 indicate that it is the greater volume of weaving and not higher unit earnings which accounts for the high daily earnings of Konya weavers. Daily and annual weaving earnings are by definition the outcome of unit earnings and the volume of weaving. Thus, an explanation of the wide earnings differentials observed in tables 8 and 9 requires closer scrutiny of various factors that affect unit earnings (piece-rates) and the volume of weaving.

Piece-rates

As noted earlier, independent weavers receive a sum per carpet rather than a payment on the basis of output per 1,000 knots as in the case of the outworkers and workshop weavers. Independent weavers do not translate their earnings per carpet into unit earnings based on knots. In order to create a basis for comparison with the out-workers and workshop weavers, however, the 1,000 knot earnings are used as the measure of piece-rates in this study.

Table 8: Comparison of weaving earnings, output and time allocated to weaving by relations of production (figures represent averages)

	Independent household production (N=77)	Putting-out system (N=17)	Workshop production (N=39)	F-statistic[a]
Earnings per weaver per year (TL)	74 736[b]	39 693	120 987	20.48***
Earnings per weaving day (TL)	434	307	675	28.36***
Earnings per 1,000 knots (TL)	86	40	55	30.11***
Number of knots per weaver per year	878 029	958 383	2 186 415	57.47***
Number of knots per weaving day	5 269	8 059	12 051	130.75***
Number of weaving days per year	170	113	182	6.30**

[a] *** and ** indicate significance at 0.001 and 0.01 per cent levels. In the following discussion, the F-statistic refers to the summary statistic of the difference in means test.

[b] US$1 = 223 Turkish liras (TL) in 1983.

Piece-rates are affected by a number of inter-related factors: the type of carpet woven, the extent of competition for labour among merchants and intermediaries, the geographic location of the village, the concentration of weaving in a given village and region, and the availability of agricultural incomes.

Export carpets command higher piece-rates relative to carpets sold on the domestic market. The average piece-rate of carpets sold exclusively in the low-income domestic market is TL 42, as opposed to an average of TL 79 for those that are predominantly exported. Among export carpets, contrary to expectations, higher knot density carpets command lower piece-rates than lower knot density carpets. The

Table 9: Average daily and unit earnings by case study village
          (in Turkish liras)

Village	N	Daily earnings from weaving[a]	Earnings per 1,000 knots	Alternative wage rate[b]
Afyon	11	270	35	250
Isparta-1,2	20	433	43	400-500
Döşemealtı	14	542	131	900[c]
Sındırgı'	15	569	86	550
Konya-1,2	24	827	63	-
Milas	15	336	102	500
Niğde-1	19	237	46	600-700
Niğde-2	15	522	77	-
Average	133[d]	488	71	

[a] Since daily earnings from weaving are not standardised in terms of weaving intensity or length of the weaving day, caution should be exercised in making comparisons among villages, as well as with wage rates from agricultural fieldwork.

[b] Daily wages in seasonal agricultural fieldwork for women; includes one meal.

[c] Piece-rates in cotton harvest in neighbouring villages can yield up to TL 900 per day.

[d] Total.

average piece-rate of the finest group of carpets (produced in Konya and Isparta workshops) is TL 54, while the lower knot density carpets command an average piece-rate of TL 98. The latter group of carpets are the Anatolian carpets produced by independent producers in Döşemealtı, Sındırgı, Milas and Niğde-2 villages. These producers undertake some ancillary weaving-related tasks described above, and unit earnings for the carpets they produce may thus command an extra premium. The average piece-rate of carpets produced in Döşemealtı, Sındırgı, Milas and Nigde-2 villages are presented in the third column of table 9. These are the highest piece-rates among sample villages, and combined with the fact that a high proportion of the independent producers sampled weave these carpets, they account for the high average piece-rate of independent producers in table 8.

Competition for labour exerts an upward pressure on piece-rates. For example, the same type of carpet produced in workshops commands a lower piece-rate in Isparta villages than in Konya villages due to the monopsonistic power of regionally based merchants in Isparta villages. The relative isolation of a village, which renders it accessible to fewer merchants as well as limiting access of the producer households to information on piece-rates, exerts a downward pressure on piece-rates.

In the literature on the forms of women's participation in paid work, two related arguments posit that women's paid work in the home is disadvantageous to them in terms of earnings. One argument is that those who work at home are not identified as workers but as "housewives", and that their paid work appears as a "spare time" activity. Therefore, homeworkers are paid at lower rates than workers that work outside the home. Secondly, it is argued that the isolation and dispersion of homeworkers allows earnings differentials among them to emerge and persist (Mies, 1982; Longhurst, 1982; Roldán, 1985).

In the case of carpet weavers, neither argument holds good. To the extent that weavers produce the same type of carpet where the putting-out system and workshop weaving coexist, the piece-rates are uniform. Secondly, home weavers, as independent producers or out-workers, are not isolated to such an extent that they are unable to compare piece-rates. This can be attributed to the concentration of weaving in the villages studied. In these villages, almost all women in a given age group are carpet weavers. Thus, regardless of the labour process, weaving schedule, age and experience of the weaver, piece-rates are the same for all weavers who weave the same carpet in a given village. Similarly, within a weaving region, piece-rate differentials are short-lived. Information on piece-rates are rapidly transmitted through local markets. Probably the key factor in the rapid equalisation of piece-rates is the interest men have in carpet prices and piece-rates by virtue of their control over the earnings and marketing. It is conceivable, however, that in larger rural settlements where weavers are not as concentrated as in small village communities, piece-rate differentials can be successfully introduced and maintained by merchants and employers. Likewise, regional separation allows piece-rate differentials across regions to persist, as the lower piece-rates of Isparta weavers relative to Konya weavers noted above indicate. In both regions weaving is concentrated, yet regional separation does not allow the piece-rate differential to be noticed by weavers and their household members.

Regional separation also operates to the disadvantage of the few Niğde-1 weavers who have recently switched from independent production to the putting-out system. These weavers are paid a per carpet sum rather than a rate per 1,000 knots. In this case, weavers do not think in terms of earnings per 1,000 knots and when earnings are expressed on a per carpet basis they often turn out to be lower than those paid on the basis of the 1,000 knot wage for the same carpet in other regions. Moreover, these weavers possess the skills of setting up the warp and consider the task an integral part of weaving. The per carpet sum covers not only weaving, but also setting up the warp and the wear and tear of the loom, if the household loom is used. Thus, their regional isolation puts these weavers in a particularly disadvantageous position in terms of earnings.

The availability of alternative sources of income, particularly the rural household's ability to secure its subsistence from agriculture, also affects piece-rates. At the individual household level, the independent producer household's need to sell a carpet as soon as possible and the local dealer's knowledge of this fact lower or keep in check the per carpet sum, and hence the piece-rate. At the village level, similar forces appear to operate. A comparison of average piece-rates of comparable carpets produced in the Nigde-2 and Döşemealtı villages (see table 9, column 3) indicates that the Döşemealtı piece-rate is almost twice as high as the Nigde-2 piece-rate. The fact that vegetable production provides year-round incomes for the majority of households in the Döşemealtı village, as opposed to the prominent landlessness of Nigde-2, suggests that the lack of access to agricultural incomes may account for the piece-rate differential between the two villages.

Alternatively, one could expect a positive relationship between piece-rates and alternative wage rates for women's work in agriculture, since the two activities would compete for women's labour time. Given the alternative employment opportunities in sample villages, however, no systematic relationship between the two variables can be posited. In most villages the demand for labour is seasonal and on a limited scale, and wage work in agriculture is not a viable income-earning alternative for the majority of weavers. As expected, a cursory examination of the third and fourth columns of table 9 does not reveal any relationship between average piece-rates and agricultural wage rates.

This discussion suggests that piece-rates are not responsive to individual characteristics of weavers but are largely determined by factors beyond their control. We shall now discuss the differences in labour input, and therefore carpet output, of weavers with particular reference to the social organisation of production and the reproductive responsibilities of weavers.

The volume of weaving

Annual carpet output of weavers is by definition the outcome of time devoted to weaving and productivity during that period. The social organisation of production or the weaving labour process is the major determinant of differences in output among weavers. Table 10 compares the average output, income and time devoted to weaving by labour process, with independent producers and outworkers grouped as home weavers. On both a daily and an annual basis, the output and earnings of workshop weavers are substantially higher than those of home weavers. The mean daily output of workshop weavers is twice as high as that of home-based weavers, reflecting the faster pace of weaving. Only this faster pace results in daily earnings that are on a par with the minimum wage. Although the average daily earnings of workshop weavers reported in table 10 appear to be above the comparable minimum wage rate in the economy in 1983 (TL 356-540),[5] when the length of the weaving day is controlled for, they turn out to be at par with the minimum wage (TL 527).

It is the higher rate of weaving and not the greater number of weaving days that accounts for the greater output of workshop weavers. Table 11 shows the distribution of annual weaving days of workshop and home weavers separately. The average number of weaving days do not significantly differ between home and workshop weaving (see table 10), but it is important to take into account the fact that for home weavers weaving days do not always reflect full-time weaving. The daily weaving schedule of the home weaver often includes a number of interruptions, although her typical weaving day may extend from sunrise to sunset.[6] The irregular weaving schedules of home weavers are reflected both in the annual and daily weaving output in table 10. Time devoted to weaving can be more accurately measured in workshops due to the regular working schedules, which means that the reported average daily output of workshop weavers closely reflects their productivity on a typical weaving day.

Table 10: Comparison of weaving earnings, output and time allocated to weaving by labour process (figures represent averages)

	Home (N=94)	Workshop (N=39)	t-statistic[a]
Earnings per weaver per year (TL)	68 398	120 987	5.65***
Earnings per weaving day (TL)	411	675	7.0***
Earnings per 1,000 knots (TL)	78	55	3.82**
Number of knots per weaver per year	892 561	2 186 415	10.74***
Number of knots per weaving day	5 774	12 051	14.23***
Number of weaving days per year	159	182	1.71

[a] *** and ** indicate significance at 0.001 and 0.01 per cent levels. t-statistic refers to the summary statistic of the difference in means test.

Table 11: Days devoted to weaving per year by home and workshop
weavers

Number of days	Home		Workshop	
	N	%	N	%
25-50	7	7.4	-	-
51-100	13	13.8	6	15.4
101-150	25	26.6	4	10.3
151-200	26	27.7	8	20.5
201-250	11	11.7	17	43.6
251-300	9	9.6	4	10.3
301-330	3	3.2	-	-
Total	94	100.0	39	100.0

Note: Totals may not add up exactly, owing to rounding.

The effect of the weaving
labour process

We shall now discuss the daily operation of workshops and
illustrate how various social practices in the workplace are effective
in raising weaving intensity and increasing the amount of time devoted
to weaving. In a nutshell, in a system where there is no direct
supervision in the workplace and workers are paid on a piece-rate
basis, the extension of familial control over women's labour into
the workplace, incentives for weavers and the divisions among weavers
interact to secure the continuity of weaving in workshops. As the
following discussion will show, the weaver's subordinate position
in the gender and age hierarchies of her household and within the
larger kinship network is effective in ensuring the successful operation of workshops. The alliance between the workshop owner and the
weaver's male relative due to their kinship ties is strengthened by
mutual financial benefits resulting from the weaver's work and is
important in both the recruitment of labour and enforcement of work
discipline. The senior man in the household makes the labour power of
the weaver available for work in the intermediary's workshop, often
in return for wage advances. The weaver is obliged to work by the
requirements of her position in the family. Senior household members
and workshop operators are also united in their opposition to changes
in established work schedules and make efforts to reduce absenteeism
and interruptions in work schedules.

In Konya workshops, the daily work schedule is regulated by the
morning and evening prayer calls, and in Isparta workshops hours vary
seasonally. This means that in Konya villages the length of the
weaving day changes daily and, excluding the lunch break, reaches 13
hours in the summer, dropping to a low of eight hours in the winter.

39

In Isparta villages, the length of the weaving day is set at eight hours during winter months and ten hours in the summer. On average, workshop weavers in Konya and Isparta villages spend 9.6 hours a day weaving.[7] Given the knot density of the weave, depending on the season, it takes between 20 and 30 days for four weavers to weave an eight-square metre carpet. Until a carpet is completed, workshop weavers weave full time, taking only Sundays off in Konya and one or two days a week off in Isparta villages.

The co-operative nature of weaving plays an important role in enforcing regular weaving schedules and minimising interruptions. Weavers of a loom have to start and stop weaving at the same time each day, and maintain the same pace of weaving in order to synchronise the completion of knots on a given row. Moreover, the payment system imparts rigidity to work schedules. As noted earlier, workshop weavers are either paid a lump sum in advance or after the completion of the carpet, or they receive their wages on a weekly basis. The former practice is prevalent in Konya workshops, while Isparta weavers receive weekly payments or smaller sums as advances. The weekly payment system is based on a daily accounting of each worker's output by the workshop operators or their daughters. This accounting system allows workers to take days off, although on a given day the rate of weaving is regulated by the collective pace at the loom. Under the lump-sum payment system, on the other hand, taking a day off means that the weaver in question owes the weaving of her share of knots or its money equivalent to others at the loom. Because incurring debts of this kind is not permitted by senior household members, the weaver has no flexibility in taking a day off until the carpet is completed. To avoid indebtedness of individual weavers to others at the loom, workers at a loom tend to belong to the same household so that substitution of labour or collective interruption of weaving is not disruptive of inter- and intra-family relations.

The institutionalisation of different payment systems in the two regions of workshop weaving can be traced to differences in the structure of the industry and the agrarian structure. In Konya villages, intense inter-merchant competition sustains an advance system in the recruitment of labour. Weavers are transferred from one workshop to another depending on the size of advances offered by respective workshop operators. In Isparta villages, on the other hand, local merchants who control a large number of looms in the region dampen the competitive pressures in control over labour and prevent the establishment of the advance system. Furthermore, as will be discussed in the next chapter, the labour requirements of agriculture in each region help sustain the respective payment systems. The agricultural work responsibilities of most weavers in Isparta villages necessitate a payment system which allows workers to take days off, whereas Konya weavers have virtually no competing work responsibilities in agriculture. The narrower age range of Isparta weavers, noted earlier, and their lower average age, is also attributable to the wider range of tasks that women in this region have to undertake and therefore an earlier retreat of women from weaving to undertake these tasks.

40

In the workshops, weavers of different looms typically compete with each other to complete carpets earlier. Such competition is encouraged by senior household members, who point out cases where carpets are completed in a shorter period of time, but weavers themselves are enthusiastic participants in the competition because they regard it as a form of amusement. In Konya villages, this competition often runs along kinship lines, since weavers of a loom are usually members of the same household or kin group. Thus the competition reinforces kinship allegiances and hinders the development of solidarity among workers in the workshop. At the same time, it raises the intensity of weaving, thus lowering the average amount of time in which carpets of a certain size are completed.

Another practice that raises both weaving intensity and the amount of time devoted to weaving is what is locally called the "pocket money carpet" practice. In recent years, the intermediaries who run the Konya workshops have instituted this practice with the agreement of weavers' male kin in order to reduce the amount of time taken off in between each carpet. Accordingly, the weaver is given the option of keeping her earnings if she weaves for a week during the ten-day break customarily taken after the completion of each carpet. The carpet, a portion of which the worker weaves during her break, is called "the pocket money carpet". The incentive of allowing weavers to keep a portion of their earnings is effective in lengthening the number of days per year devoted to weaving, as well as in raising the daily rate of weaving. Although the practice virtually eliminates any leisure time weavers might have, weavers work with more enthusiasm on the "pocket money carpet". The greater output and earnings generated in a week become instantly known in the community, however, and as in the case of inter-loom rivalries for earlier completion of carpets, it constitutes a pretext for senior household members to pressure the weaver to work as productively on regular carpets as well.

The foregoing discussion of the daily operation of workshops reveals how the pre-existing controls over women are embedded in and extended by the expansion of wage labour in workshops. This discussion suggests that once women become wage workers outside the home and a sharp division between weaving and other kinds of tasks is established, then there is more occasion to intensify pressures to generate as much output as possible during the period of time set aside for weaving. Regional differences in the extent to which workshop weaving becomes a compulsion are attributable to the characteristics of the agrarian structure to be taken up in the next chapter.

The effect of reproductive responsibilities

In this section we shall examine the interaction of reproductive responsibilities and weaving work, by exploring the effect of the differing responsibilities of weavers on their ability to earn. The content of reproductive tasks varies by household economic standing and by region. For instance, in some regions bread bought from the village baker supplements the bread that is periodically baked at home, while in other regions women bake bread daily. In the case study villages, women are almost totally responsible for reproductive tasks. These tasks are child care, food preparation and cooking, cleaning, sewing, mending, knitting, fetching water and firewood, preparing dung patties for fuel, milking and feeding household animals. There are few exceptions to the norm: men in Sındırgı and Milas villages may also feed household animals and fetch water, if women are unable to do so due to more pressing tasks. In addition, in Sındırgı and Isparta-2 villages where firewood is used for fuel and must be gathered at long distances outside the village, the task is undertaken by men.

In the absence of time budget data, in this section two household composition variables are used as proxy variables to gauge the extent of the weavers' reproductive responsibilities: having young children and having assistance in the household. We examine the effect of having young children and the counteracting effect of having assistance in the household on weaving output and the choice of the weaving labour process. The following questions are posed: What are the demographic characteristics of home and workshop weavers? Are women with assistance from other women in their household more likely to weave in workshops? Are those with young children more likely to weave at home? Does workshop weaving usher in changes in the sexual division of labour as regards reproductive responsibilities?

Compared to home weavers, workshop weavers are on average younger (22 years versus 28 years), and a greater proportion of workshop weavers have assistance from women in their household (82 per cent of workshop weavers as opposed to 38 per cent of home weavers). It is difficult to determine whether women with young children are more likely to weave in their homes, relative to weavers who have no young children. For most weavers there is no choice between home and workshop weaving. The appropriate sample to explore the relationship between the incidence of having young children and the weaving labour process is the group of married, divorced and widowed weavers in Konya and Isparta villages where the two labour processes co-exist. Yet restricting the sample in this manner renders its size too small to establish a statistically meaningful association. None the less, among this group of weavers a greater proportion of women with children under the age of 5[8] weave in workshops compared to women who have no dependent children (84.6 per cent versus 66.7 per cent). This can be explained by the availability of assistance from non-weaver women in the household or help from non-resident female kin. Fifty-two per cent of Konya and 30 per cent of Isparta workshop weavers belong to extended family households, and in both villages over 70 per cent of weavers have access to help from non-weaver women in the household. Extended family households are more likely to have a division of labour among weaver and non-weaver women, because they embody a greater number of adult women. This division of labour facilitates workshop weaving and is conducive to achieving a greater output, regardless of the weaving labour process. In the absence of an extended family household organisation, as the following discussion will show, women with young children relegate child care to women from their natal household, with virtually no change in the sexual division of labour in the weaver's household.

Isparta and Konya villages display different patterns in the way that workshop weavers combine weaving with the care of young children. In both sets of villages, pre-natal abstinence from weaving work is virtually non-existent; indeed, in Konya workshops weaving is interrupted when delivery actually begins. While in Konya workshops women resume weaving in the workshop within 15 days to a month after delivery, in Isparta villages the post-natal break from weaving is longer. Given the almost immediate return to workshop weaving in Konya villages to ensure the continuity of weaving, infants are brought to the workshop to be nursed by their mothers a number of times during the weaving day. While the mother is nursing, the woman who brings the child continues the weaving. This is usually the mother, mother-in-law or unmarried sister of the weaver. In Isparta villages, weavers with young children weave smaller carpets at home for a few years. When Isparta weavers resume weaving in the workshop they entrust the care of young children to older siblings and in winter months may bring their children along to the workshop, whereas in Konya villages the care of children is relegated to older siblings and non-weaver women. As for domestic chores, workshop weavers perform these in the evening or on their days off. Chores other than those that have immediacy (such as milking or child care) are not relegated to the mother-in-law, although the mothers of single women perform these tasks (such as cooking and cleaning). A few Konya weavers who live in nuclear households and whose husbands are seasonal construction workers reported that in winter months and if they are home anyway, their husbands mind the young children. Otherwise, the weaver has to find a relative from her natal household to take care of the children. When asked if their husbands helped in any other household chores, one weaver noted that her husband made tea for breakfast in the summer,[9] but that help in other chores was not forthcoming. Thus, the overall workload of married weavers, especially those who live in nuclear households, is particularly heavy.

Turning to the sample as a whole, we can now examine the effects of having assistance in reproductive tasks and of having young children on weavers' output. Whether measured on a daily or an annual basis, table 12 shows that on average weaving output of principal weavers increases with the availability of help in the household. Assistance is assured by the presence of women in the household who are neither weavers nor students.

Annual and daily output figures in table 13 indicate that weavers with children under the age of 5 produce more relative to those with no young children. This anomalous result could be explained by weavers' access to assistance in child care or by the greater incidence of workshop weavers among those with young children, or by both.

Table 12: Principal weavers' output by availability of assistance in the household[a]

Number of women in household[a]	N	Annual output[b]	Daily output[b]
0	65	982 109	6 385
1	55	1 544 675	8 635
2	13	1 567 438	9 445
F-statistic		7.91	8.14
Significance level		0.0006	0.0005

[a] Women and girls above the age of 12, who are neither weavers nor students.

[b] Average number of knots.

Controlling for access to help in the household, in table 14 we observe that having young children is associated with significantly higher output among weavers who have no assistance. Similarly, among those who have assistance, weavers with young children generate a greater output on average, although the differences are not statistically significant.

Table 13: Weaving output of principal weavers[a] by presence of children under the age of 5

	N	Annual output[b]	Daily output[b]
Weavers without children under 5	44	998 215	6 446
Weavers with children under 5	35	1 309 466	8 047
t-statistic		1.88	2.11
Significance level		(0.0438)	(0.0382)

[a] Excludes single women.

[b] Average number of knots.

The definition of the "help variable" may account for the statistically significant positive association between having young children and high output among women who have no assistance in the

44

Table 14: Weaving output of principal weavers[a] by presence of children under the age of 5 and availability of assistance in the household[b]

	Has no assistance (N=60)		Has assistance (N=19)	
	Has no child (N=32)	Has child (N=28)	Has no child (N=12)	Has child (N=7)
Annual output[c]	859 113	1 173 262	1 369 155	1 854 283
t-statistic[d]	1.85 (0.069)		1.24 (0.233)	
Daily output[c]	5 664	7 486	8 529	10 289
t-statistic[d]	2.32 (0.024)		1.04 (0.312)	

[a] Excludes single women.

[b] Women and girls above the age of 12 who are neither weavers nor students.

[c] Average number of knots.

[d] Significance levels are reported in parentheses.

household. As noted above, assistance may not necessarily be confined to household members. First, some women with dependent children have assistance from female kin who are not members of the household. These women now appear in the category who do not have help and may thereby introduce an upward bias in average output figures. Second, it is possible that the weaving labour process might modify this two-way breakdown of output: in the sample, weavers with young children could be concentrated in villages of workshop weaving where overall output tends to be higher. Thus, their higher output may reflect the effect of workshop weaving and not that of having young children per se. Yet this possibility cannot be explored here since the sample size is too small to control further for the effects of home and workshop weaving in table 14. We can, however, explore whether having young children makes a difference in terms of output, when the weaving labour process is controlled for. In table 15 we observe that, among workshop weavers, having young children makes almost no difference in terms of both daily and annual output. This is to be expected since weavers conform to the pace of workshop weaving whether or not they have young children. Only in Isparta workshops is absenteeism possible, and this would be reflected in lower annual output, but it does not seem to affect the average annual output figure in table 15. Similarly, among home weavers, having young children is not associated with lower output. This result is expected as well, since home weaving is not expected to be in conflict with the care of young children.

Table 15: Weaving output of principal weavers[a] by presence of children under the age of 5 and labour process

	Home weaving (N=62)		Workshop weaving (N=17)	
	Has no child (N=38)	Has child (N=24)	Has no child (N=6)	Has child (N=11)
Annual output[b]	873 835	1 078 474	1 785 960	1 813 449
t-statistic[c]	1.24 (0.2180)		0.07 (0.9453)	
Daily output[b]	5 503	6 537	12 417	11 339
t-statistic[c]	1.53 (0.1310)		1.29 (0.2152)	

[a] Excludes single women.

[b] Average number of knots.

[c] Significance levels are reported in parentheses.

From the sample, the conclusion may be drawn that both having assistance and having young children are associated with the greater average output of principal weavers. Even when availability of household assistance is controlled for, those weavers with young children who have no help generate greater output than weavers with no young children. Among both home and workshop weavers, on the other hand, having young children is not associated with statistically significant differences in output. Thus, there is no evidence that having young children has a negative effect on output or restricts women to home weaving.

The foregoing discussion indicates that the expected conflict between reproductive responsibilities and weaving employment is modified by two factors in the case of rural carpet weavers. First, across the sample, the lack of workshop weaving and other kinds of paid work for women implies that those who weave at home are not only women with dependent children, but also single young women and older women with relatively fewer competing reproductive responsibilities. Second, the availability of informal child-care networks, whether from non-weaver women in the household or from female kin who are not household members, reduces the incompatibility of workshop weaving with having young children and makes workshop weaving possible for women with dependent children.

Weaving history of weavers

Open-ended interviews reveal that for most of the weavers weaving is a lifetime activity. Once they start weaving, most weave continuously for 20 to 25 years, although their output level may fluctuate over the life cycle. Assuming that the weaver starts knotting and learning other weaving skills at the age of 12, in the first year after she starts weaving her output will be low, reflecting the slow speed of knotting. Within a couple of years she becomes an experienced weaver and her speed reaches that customary for the village. The highest weaving output of her weaving history, albeit with fluctuations, is during the period up to 20 years after she begins weaving. After this period, weaving may become intermittent, depending on the number of daughters the weaver has and the weaving labour process. If she has at least two daughters, then she is likely to relegate weaving work sooner than if she has only one daughter or only sons. In the latter cases, especially if weaving is carried out at home, the weaver maintains her pace of weaving until her daughter marries or daughter(s)-in-law join the household. Thus, the customary age of "retirement" from weaving is somewhere between the ages of 35 and 45.

In 1983, the average number of years spent in weaving was 13 years. Forty-five per cent of sample weavers had been weaving for over ten years, with 20 per cent weaving for more than 20 years. Almost two-thirds of sample weavers are married, divorced or widowed, and in 1983 on average this group of weavers had been weaving for 17.8 years, with 33 per cent weaving for over 20 years. These characteristics indicate that, contrary to the claims of those who argue for the exemption of weaving work from the coverage of the SSL, weavers do not give up weaving after marriage. As noted above, weavers typically reduce the amount of weaving or give up when another weaver in the household begins weaving on a full-time basis.

There is considerable stability in the weaving employment of sample weavers, which is largely a reflection of the limited choice of weavers over the relations of production. The most common pattern is to have woven as an independent producer throughout the weaving tenure (table 16). Only 15 per cent have shifted among different relations of production during their weaving history. Similarly, the mode is always to have woven at home (table 17). Only 11.3 per cent have shifted between workshop and home weaving.

A review of the reasons for occupational changes on the part of the weaver (change of employer and/or labour process) reveals the perceptions, motives and reactions of weavers and their households in the context of the development of carpet weaving in the village. This review also provides insights on the extent to which weavers themselves decide on changes.

The weavers who have made the greatest number of changes in their weaving history are those who have switched among different workshops, and between the putting-out system and workshop weaving.

The weaving histories of workshop weavers reveal that the most common reason motivating a change of workshop is the existence of an

earnings differential between two workshops. The greatest number of
such changes have occurred in Konya villages in response to the
large sums obtained as wage advances by male kin of weavers. As soon
as an advance is obtained, the weaver is instructed to resume weaving
in a different workshop, at which she weaves until the debt is paid.
On the other hand, Isparta weavers reported that slow adjustment of
piece-rates provides the pretext for a change of workshop. Moreover,
some Konya weavers stated that, if there is absenteeism and low
intensity of weaving in their present workshop, they are instructed
by their male kin to switch to another workshop.

Table 16:   Distribution of sample weavers by pattern of changes
            in employer

	N	%
Always an independent weaver	60	45.1
Always a merchant-controlled[a] weaver	52	39.0
Started out as independent weaver, ended up as merchant-controlled weaver	14	10.6
Started out/ended up as merchant-controlled weaver[b]	1	0.8
Started out/ended up as independent weaver[c]	6	4.5
Total	133	100.0

[a] "Merchant-controlled weaver" refers to both the putting-out system
and workshop weavers.

[b] Worked as an independent weaver in between.

[c] Worked for a merchant in between.

In addition to financial motives for changing workshops, a
large number of changes by Konya weavers were caused by the closing
of workshops. Workshops typically close down because the operator
cannot finance wage advances and therefore cannot control a sufficient number of weavers to keep the workshop in operation.

An equally large number of switches among Konya workshops were
motivated by kinship obligations. When a relative begins operating
a workshop, his female relatives often switch to working in his workshop. This switch is expected to result in large wage advances in
the course of time.

A change in residence of the weaver, due to marriage or separation from an extended family residence, results in a change of workshop in both regions. Generally, if the new residence is too far
from the initial workshop, then a closer workshop is sought. In Konya

villages, in addition to a change of workshop, the marriage of a workshop weaver also brings about her indebtedness to a workshop owner, from whom her father-in-law has obtained wage advances to finance her wedding expenses. The advance is obtained with the promise that the bride will resume weaving in the workshop of the intermediary who extends the sum. Thus, the workshop where the weaver is to work is predetermined at marriage.

Table 17: Distribution of sample weavers by pattern of changes in labour process

	N	%
Always a home weaver	87	65.4
Always a workshop weaver	31	23.3
Shifts between home and workshop weaving:		
- workshop to home	5	3.8
- home to workshop	4	3.0
- home to home[a]	2	1.5
- workshop to workshop[a]	4	3.0
Total	133	100.0

[a] Worked in the other labour process in between.

Lastly, a few changes of workshop were caused by discord among weavers in a workshop or between the male kin of the weaver and the intermediary.

As for the shifts between the putting-out system and workshop weaving, the primary reasons are related to changing domestic responsibilities of weavers. As noted in the previous section, if a weaver with an infant does not have any female relative to whom she can relegate child care during the weaving day, then she stops weaving in the workshop until such time as the conflict between workshop weaving and child care is resolved. The changing household division of labour, which results from changing household composition, also affects the choice of labour process. In the Konya and Isparta villages, the recent practice of making a per carpet payment to out-workers, noted earlier, makes home weaving attractive provided there is a sufficient number of women in the household. The loss of household weavers through marriage, however, forces the sole weaver left behind to start weaving in a workshop. In this case, the sole weaver in the family is unable to maintain the pace of weaving without the co-operation of another weaver, and earnings generated by her weaving at home do not match those possible in a workshop.

In Isparta villages, there exists some fluidity between workshop production and the putting-out system. In between carpets woven at home, weavers weave a number of days at a workshop. Some weaving histories in Isparta villages also reveal that, during periods of growth in carpet demand (produced for the domestic market), out-workers switched to independent production. This fluidity, when the weaving household switches from the putting-out system to independent production whenever the market is expanding and back when it is contracting, is observed in other regions as well (Ayata, 1982).

Finally, the weaving histories of independent weavers who switched to the putting-out system reflect the conditions under which independent production is displaced by the putting-out system. The most common reason given for the shift from independent pro-duction to weaving for a merchant is the marketing difficulties experienced by independent households in the carpets customarily produced. Either because of difficulties in selling their carpets or due to the cost of reaching the market, these families began weaving for a merchant. The shift was accompanied by a change in the type of carpet woven. The merchant introduces the weaving of the new carpet by offering a piece-rate (or the per carpet sum equivalent) that is slightly higher than the present per carpet earnings of the independent producers, but lower than the piece-rate for the new carpet in the region of intensified competition among merchants. In addition, wage advances offered by the intermediary facilitated this decision for some households. The ease of receiving dyed yarn, rather than having to dye the yarn themselves, was also attractive.

Conclusion

This chapter presented the characteristics of carpet weavers and traced the life cycle and weaving history of weavers from the time they acquire weaving skills in childhood to "retirement", with the relegation of weaving work responsibilities to younger women in the household. The discussion of relations of production revealed the almost perfect fit between weaving work and cultural ideals of what is proper for women to do under all three relations of pro-duction. Both weaving histories of weavers and the quality of work relations show that weavers have low autonomy in decisions concerning weaving employment, a finding which will be discussed in Chapter 4. The discussion of factors which determine weaving income shows that unit earnings are not responsive to individual characteristics of weavers, and in a given type of carpet within a weaving region unit earnings differentials are short-lived. The volume of weaving, on the other hand, is affected by both the weaving labour process and the stage in the weaver's life cycle, which is closely related to household composition. Workshop weavers produce more because they devote more time to weaving and weave at a higher intensity. Having young children does not negatively affect weaving output, while the availability of help from female house-hold members greatly enhances it. Availability of assistance also reduces the conflict between weaving and women's reproductive responsibilities that emerges with the separation of home and the workplace. Workshop weaving is made possible through the substitution of the labour of non-weaver women for that of weavers, as well as by weavers bearing a double workload, and not through a change in the sexual division of labour in household tasks.

Notes

[1] The 133 weavers who make up the sample are all women, and are the principal weavers in their household. The principal weaver is defined in terms of the amount of labour time devoted to weaving and her seniority to other household weavers. While there exist principal weavers below the age of 15 in the case study villages, a decision was made not to include any weavers under 15 in the sample, mainly due to the difficulty of obtaining responses to most questions in the questionnaire.

[2] The terms "family" and "household" are used interchangeably in this study, and refer to a number of people who share the same domestic unit, and who invariably have kinship ties to each other.

[3] According to a 1968 survey, the incidence of extended families in rural Turkey is 38.7 per cent. While 55.4 per cent of households are nuclear families, 5.9 per cent are dissolved or non-family households (Timur, 1981).

[4] Daily weaving earnings were calculated by dividing annual weaving earnings of each weaver by the number of days it took the principal weaver and her co-weavers to produce the annual carpet output (i.e. the number of days that elapsed between setting up the warp and the completion of each carpet).

[5] This is the legal minimum based on a 7.5-hour working day, applicable to men and women non-agricultural workers in 1983. The upper limit represents the gross wage rate, while the lower rate is the net minimum wage rate of a single worker who has no dependents and lives in a settlement of less than 5,000 persons. The actual wage rate would be closer to the upper limit if the worker were married, had children and lived in a settlement with a population greater than 5,000.

[6] It is generally the case that, once they begin weaving a carpet, home weavers devote at least some amount of time each day to weaving. Therefore, the number of days that elapse between setting up the warp and the completion of the carpet does not include days when no weaving has taken place.

[7] This average figure was arrived at by taking into consideration the variation in the length of days over the year, as well as the seasonal concentration of each worker's weaving activity.

[8] This can be considered as the age below which children are dependent on the constant attention of adults.

[9] In the summer, when the weaving days are longer, weavers take a short break after one or two hours of weaving and go home for breakfast.

CHAPTER 3

THE ECONOMIC POSITION OF THE WEAVING HOUSEHOLD

This chapter situates carpet weaving within the broader framework of agrarian transformation in rural Turkey. The dual objectives
are to examine the conditions that affect the volume of weaving and
hence weaving income, with particular reference to the position of
the household in the agrarian structure, and to evaluate the effect
of weaving income on the household's economic position.

The discussion begins with an analysis of the nature of the
agrarian structure and its relationship to carpet weaving. In
particular the analysis focuses on how the economic standing of
households (which is discussed in terms of access to land and the
magnitude of household income generated from various economic
activities) and the labour requirements in agriculture condition
the volume of carpet weaving. Analysis of the agrarian structure
is central to the discussion of the household's economic position,
due to the relative importance of agricultural incomes for weaving
households. On average, income from agricultural production
accounts for 33 per cent of total household income, following the
38 per cent share of weaving income, although across villages
there is considerable variation in the relative importance of various
components of household income. Secondly, the contribution of the
weaver to household income is assessed, and the importance of
weaving as a cash-generating activity is discussed, illustrating
the variation in the utilisation of weaving income. Thirdly, the
analysis focuses on the economic standing of households headed by
women according to household composition as identified in Chapter 2.

The agrarian structure of weaving villages

The distribution of cultivable land in property and in usufruct[1]
presented in tables 18 and 19 underscores the predominantly smallholder nature of agricultural production in the case study villages.
Twenty-six per cent of sample households do not own land. Table 18
shows that the remaining 74.4 per cent own 3.5 hectares on average,
although half of the households own less than 2 hectares. There
is no close association between the amount of land directly cultivated by households and the amount of land owned by them. In the

case study villages, landless or smallholder households gain access to land through various means: they rent or share-crop land, they jointly cultivate land with their kin who hold title to land, and a few cultivate plots lent to them by their kin. Some households relegate cultivation to share-cropper farmers in return for rent in kind. The distribution of land in usufruct, which reflects the net result of giving up and taking on cultivation of land, is shown in table 19. Excluding the 21.1 per cent of households that do not engage in cultivation, table 19 shows that 56.2 per cent of house- holds cultivate less than 2 hectares. However, the distribution of landholdings among Turkish rural households presented in the 1980 Agricultural Survey reveals that a smaller proportion of households (28.4 per cent) have access to less than 2 hectares of land (SIS, 1983).

While the majority of sample households are smallholders, the case study villages display a variety of land tenure systems. It is possible to distinguish two agrarian structures in the case study villages based on the close association between the land tenure system, crops produced and degree of mechanisation in agri- culture: (a) mechanised mono-culture grain farming with share- cropping as the predominant land tenure system, as observed in Konya-1, 2 and Niğde-2 villages; and (b) multi-crop smallholder agriculture observed in Afyon, Döşemealtı, Sındırgı, Milas, Niğde-1 and Isparta-1, 2 villages. In the following discussion the two agrarian structures are respectively referred to as mono-crop and multi-crop agriculture.

Table 18: Distribution of cultivable land in property

Hectares	N	%
0.05-0.9	20	20.2
1.0-1.9	30	30.3
2.0-2.9	13	13.1
3.0-3.9	7	7.1
4.0-4.9	4	4.0
5.0-5.9	8	8.1
6.0-6.9	7	7.1
7.0-9.9	4	4.0
10.0-25.0	6	6.1
Total	99	100.0

Mean: 3.5 hectares

In villages of mono-crop agriculture, wheat and barley are pro- duced as both subsistence and cash crops. Mechanisation in grain farming has virtually eliminated demand for labour in agriculture and has also made the cultivation of small plots too costly for owners. A few share-cropper farmers, most of whom are also large landowners, undertake cultivation on behalf of numerous smallholders. Most village households turn their land over to a share-cropper farmer, who owns agricultural machinery; the landowner and share-cropper split the costs of cultivation and the share-cropper carries out production in return for half the yield.

Table 19:   Distribution of cultivable land in usufruct

Hectares	N	%
0.05-0.9	34	32.4
1.0-1.9	25	23.8
2.0-2.9	12	11.4
3.0-3.9	8	7.6
4.0-4.9	4	3.8
5.0-5.9	6	5.7
6.0-6.9	7	6.7
7.0-9.9	2	1.9
10.0-25.0	7	6.7
Total	105	100.0

Mean: 3.1 hectares

In the Konya and Niğde-2 villages, 41 per cent of households do not own land, while 46 per cent do not engage in cultivation. If the garden plots are excluded, the latter figure rises to 76.9 per cent. There is virtually no demand for paid or unpaid labour in agriculture. If the household has access to land, women's agricultural fieldwork is limited to the care of the garden plot. Very few seasonal jobs are available in threshing, and no men from sample households engage in this work.

In villages of multi-crop agriculture, on the other hand, smallholder households produce a range of subsistence and cash crops using family labour. In contrast to mono-crop villages, only 19 per cent of households are landless and over half of these households gain access to land through various arrangements.

The composition of crops varies by village. The crops range from exclusively cash crops (tobacco, sugar beet, roses) to those that also meet part of household subsistence needs (grains, vegetables, fruits, opium poppies, sunflowers, sesame). All households that engage in cultivation gear their production to meet at least part of household consumption.

In villages of multi-crop agriculture, both men and women work in the labour-intensive agricultural tasks of planting, weeding and harvesting, which extend throughout the major part of the year. Across villages there are variations in the sexual division of labour

in agriculture. In Sındırgı, Milas and Döşemealtı villages a
flexible division of labour prevails, where men and women engage in
the same tasks but perform different labour. For example, during
the olive harvest men knock down ripe olives from trees while women
collect olives from the ground. Likewise, men prepare the soil with
hoes for tobacco planting, while women plant the tobacco seedlings
one by one. In Afyon, on the other hand, men and women perform
different tasks. While men are prominent in irrigation and sowing,
they are virtually absent in other tasks.

    In almost all villages soil preparation and sowing are mechan-
ised. Small plots in Döşemealtı and hilly terrain in Milas villages
require the use of animals in soil preparation. Likewise, in most
villages cereal harvests are mechanised. Sample households gain
access to tractors, threshers and sometimes combine harvesters
through rentals.

    Table 20 shows that weavers participate in a wide range of
tasks in agriculture.[2] Yet households rely on non-household labour
during weeding and harvesting seasons to meet labour requirements
of cash-crop farming. This demand is met by the exchange of labour
among neighbours and by hired help. Wage labour is used only if
family labour and labour through reciprocal exchanges are not
sufficient to undertake the task in question. Except for the Afyon
village, where all agricultural wage workers are women, in other
multi-crop villages wage workers are both men and women. Yet wage
work is available on a limited scale and is only a supplementary
source of household income (see table 21).[3]

Table 20: Participation of weavers in agricultural tasks by crop
           in multi-crop villages

Village	Tasks
Afyon	Weeding, harvesting sugar beet, potatoes, opium poppies, harvesting sunflowers
Isparta-1, 2	Weeding, harvesting sugar beet, potatoes, opium poppies, harvesting apples, grapes, roses, sesame
Döşemealtı	Planting, weeding and harvesting various fresh vegetables, harvesting sesame, reaping grain
Sındırgı	Planting, weeding, harvesting tobacco, harvesting sunflowers, sesame
Milas	Planting, weeding, harvesting tobacco, harvesting olives, sesame
Nigde-1	Harvesting apples, grapes

Table 21: Availability of agricultural wage work for women in the
case study villages

	N	%
No wage work available (Konya-1, 2, Niğde-2)	39	29.3
Limited wage work for older and married women (Isparta-1, 2: harvesting apples, grapes, roses; Milas: planting, weeding, harvesting tobacco, har- vesting olives; Niğde-1: harvesting, apples, grapes)	54	40.6
Limited wage work for all women (Döşemealtı: harvesting cotton in nearby villages; Sındırgı: planting, weeding, harvesting tobacco)	29	21.8
Widespread wage work avail- able for all women (Afyon: weeding, harvest- ing sugar beet, potatoes, opium poppies)	11	8.3
Total	133	100.0

The relationship between the agrarian structure and weaving

The composition of household income in mono-crop and multi-crop villages is presented in table 22. Although the magnitude of total and per adult household incomes are not significantly different between the two village groups, there is considerable difference in the absolute magnitude and relative importance of different components of household income.[4] On average, income from agricultural production is substantially lower in mono-crop villages, while incomes from weaving and other economic activities besides crop production are substantially higher in mono-crop villages than in multi-crop villages. In the case study villages, other sources of household income besides weaving and cultivation are self-employment in petty trade, services and animal husbandry, and wage work in construction, mining and agriculture. On average, weaving accounts for 50 per cent of household earnings in mono-crop villages, but only 33 per cent in multi-crop villages. Combined with income from other non-agricultural sources, the share of non-agricultural earnings reaches a high of 88 per cent of household income in mono-crop villages.

The fact that average agricultural incomes in mono-crop villages are lower than in multi-crop villages can in part be explained by the predominance of share-cropping practices in mono-crop agriculture. In addition, compared to other types of crop farming, mono-culture grain farming tends to generate less income per hectare, which is not compensated by the fact that the average size of own landholdings is greater in mono-crop than in multi-crop villages.

Table 22:   Annual household incomes from various sources and their share in total household income by agrarian structure (figures represent averages)

| | Agrarian structure | | t-statistic[a] |
	Mono-crop (N=39)	Multi-crop (N=94)	
Total household income (TL)	439 932	402 832	0.76 (0.4479)
Total household income per adult (TL)	108 887	115 599	0.402 (0.5270)
Agricultural income (TL)	70 716	183 944	3.38 (0.0010)
Weaving income (TL)	200 680	109 937	4.04 (0.0000)
Other income (TL)	168 536	108 951	2.13 (0.0352)
Share of agricultural income in total household income (%)	12	42	5.89 (0.0000)
Share of weaving income in total household income (%)	50	33	3.41 (0.0009)
Share of other income in total household income (%)	38	25	2.7 (0.0079)

[a] Significance levels are reported in parentheses.

The difference in magnitude of weaving incomes between the two types of agrarian structure is largely due to the substantial difference in the volume of weaving. Table 23 shows the difference in mean annual weaving output and earnings of the principal weavers in the two types of agrarian structure. Weavers in mono-crop villages produce and earn almost twice as much as weavers in villages of multi-crop agriculture. Economic pressures and the absence of demands on women's labour in agriculture are compelling factors affecting the volume of weaving in mono-crop villages. Acute landlessness and dependence of households on weaving income due to the inadequacy of incomes from alternative sources generate pressures to increase weaving output. The mechanised nature of crop production facilitates a greater amount of weaving by women, since women have no work responsibilities in agriculture.

Table 23: Annual weaving output and income of principal weaver by agrarian structure
(figures represent averages)

	Agrarian structure		t-statistic[a]
	Mono-crop (N=39)	Multi-crop (N=94)	
Output (knots)	1 813 993	1 047 076	5.08 (0.0000)
Income (TL)	121 663	68 118	5.77 (0.0000)

[a] Significance levels are reported in parentheses.

The relative importance of weaving income for households in mono-crop villages is observed once again in table 24. When annual household weaving income is ranked among household income categories, mono-crop village households are seen to be more likely to have weaving as the primary and secondary source of household income as compared to households of multi-crop villages.

Under both agrarian structures, women in households with greater agricultural incomes weave less, but the inverse relationship between agricultural income and weaving output and income should not be exaggerated: for the sample as a whole, for every TL100,000 increase in earnings from crop production, weaving income is estimated to fall by TL17,260.[5] The weak response of weaving output to household earnings from agriculture implies that women in wealthier households do not weave substantially less than women in poorer households. This finding may be explained by the close association of carpet weaving with women's socially constructed role in rural Turkey. It also suggests that weaving income may not be solely used for basic subsistence in rural households. Hence, we turn to the examination of the effects of weaving income on household economic position.

Table 24: Importance of weaving income by agrarian structure

Ranking of annual household weaving income among household income categories[a]	Agrarian structure			
	Mono-crop		Multi-crop	
	N	%	N	%
Primary income	18	46.2	27	28.7
Secondary income	20	51.3	37	39.4
Tertiary income	1	2.6	30	31.9
	39	100.0	94	100.0

Chi-square: 13.58
Significance: 0.0011

[a] Ranking is based on a comparison of three components of household income: income from agricultural production; weaving income; incomes from other sources, i.e. petty trade, services, animal husbandry, wage income.

Note: Totals may not add up exactly owing to rounding.

The role of weaving income

This section assesses the importance of weaving income for rural households in quantitative terms as well as its effects on the economic position of households. The principal weaver's weaving income accounts for 26 per cent of total household income on average. Sixty-three per cent of weavers generate weaving incomes that account for less than one-fourth of household income and in 9 per cent of sample households this contribution constitutes more than 50 per cent of household income. In addition, in 18 per cent of households, the weaving earnings of the principal weaver alone are greater than the total earnings of the household from other income sources. As stated in the introduction to this chapter, weaving income generated by all household weavers constitutes 38 per cent of household income on average, and in 26.3 per cent of households this share exceeds the total non-weaving income of the household.

The relationship of the absolute magnitude and relative importance of weaving income to total household income is presented in table 25, where the weaving income contributions of both the principal weaver and all household weavers are reported. As total household

60

income increases, the absolute magnitude of weaving income rises, while its relative importance declines. For principal weavers, the average contribution drops from 42 to 14 per cent, while the share of total weaving income in household income drops from 49 to 28 per cent as household income increases. The drop in the relative contribution accompanying the increase in household income indicates that other components of household income rise faster than earnings from weaving. Indeed, the share of income from crop production increases from an average share of 27 to 42 per cent, while the share of "other" income does not significantly differ by household income strata reported in table 25.

Table 25: Weaving income by household income category
(figures represent averages)

Household income category (TL)	N	Weaving income of principal weaver (TL)	Prop.1[a] (%)	Total weaving income (TL)	Prop.2[b] (%)
44,200-224,500	33	59 348	42	68 222	49
226,000-353,500	33	75 431	27	114 982	41
354,000-550,000	33	98 490	23	150 241	35
560,000-1,400,000	34	101,472	14	210 498	28
F-statistic		4.89	14.35	11.09	4.16
Significance level		0.0030	0.0000	0.0000	0.0075

[a] Share of principal weaver's weaving income in total household income.

[b] Share of weaving income generated by all household weavers in total household income.

The above figures on the share of weaving income in household income can only partially capture the importance of weaving income. First, the shares reported underestimate the relative importance of weaving income in cash receipts, since total household income includes the value of subsistence production imputed at market prices.[6] Secondly, quantitative measurement alone does not capture the immediate and dynamic effects of weaving income.

Expenditure patterns vary among villages. Weavers state that weaving income is spent on non-durable and durable consumption goods, their own or their daughters' dowry (which consists of goods that will furnish the home), wedding and educational expenses of brothers and sons, construction of houses, agricultural inputs, cultivable land, tractors, trucks, pilgrimage trips of family elders to Mecca,

all-male vacations and other conspicuous consumption by men.
In general, the particular spending pattern and the effect of
weaving income on household economic position depend not only on the
initial economic position of the household as measured by income and
productive assets, but also on the magnitude of weaving earnings,
the size of each weaving income payment and the possibilities for
investment.

It is the receipt of weaving income in lump-sum payments that
enables the purchase of expensive consumer durables or means of
production. Men obtain lump-sum payments by using weaving labour
power either as "collateral" to obtain credit or as a means of saving.

The first practice is seen in the Konya region of workshop
weaving, where large sums are obtained as advances on wages by male
household members. The wage advances are paid back through the
weaving of household weavers in the course of one to two years.
Purchases of expensive durables by weaving households are less
common in the Isparta villages, where workshop weavers are paid
weekly. Among independent weaving households, the use of weaving
labour power as collateral is more informal. Relying on future
household weaving earnings, household members make credit purchases,
which are subsequently paid back through the sale of carpets.

The second practice of using carpets as a way of saving is a
pattern observed among independent weaving households. As stated
in Chapter 2, some independent producers in the Milas, Döşemealtı,
Sındırgı and Niğde-2 villages do not immediately sell the carpets
they have produced, and therefore obtain large sums from the sale
of a number of carpets at given intervals. To be able to continue
weaving without selling carpets, however, largely depends on the
household's economic position, and whether or not the subsistence
of the household is ensured through landholdings and animals.

In general, weaving income has two kinds of effects on the
economic position of rural households: (a) it contributes to the
subsistence of the household; and (b) it makes household accumulation possible.

The first effect of weaving income is observed among both
prosperous and poor households. Among near landless households in
the Niğde-1 and Afyon villages, low annual weaving income generated
in the production of carpets geared to the low-income domestic
market can only reproduce the household at its present subsistence
level.

For smallholder peasant households in villages of multi-crop
agriculture, weaving in the non-agricultural season provides cash
income that enables the household to subsist until the sale of the
cash crop. In this case, weaving income prevents the indebtedness
of the peasant household, by bridging the discrete intervals between
receipts from agricultural production. Through weaving, the smallholder peasant household also hedges against the risks of crop
failure or delays in the receipt of proceeds from the sale of cash
crops. Typically, cash crops such as tobacco and sugar beet are
bought by the State and the proceeds may not be received by the
household until up to eight months after the sale. In such

circumstances, weaving income allows the household both to subsist and purchase the agricultural inputs for the new planting season.

In Konya and Niğde-2 villages, weaving income alleviates pressures for migration and prevents full-scale proletarianisation. In these regions, young women in landless households are full-time weavers who support their households through weaving, while most young men are unemployed. Since both men and women consider the activity to be women's work, and weaving secures a basic level of household subsistence, men are not pressured to take up weaving or to migrate in search of work. At most, these men work as seasonal construction workers in the village. The decision of men not to migrate is most probably shaped by the magnitude of urban unemployment in Turkey in the 1980s and is not based solely on the existence of weaving incomes generated by their female kin. To the extent that it is men who migrate and women who weave, however, the slowing down of rural migration means that the workload of rural men relative to women is declining over time. As is often claimed in policy debates on the promotion of the carpet industry, the expansion of carpet weaving indeed provides employment in rural areas and may prevent rural-urban migration depending on the agrarian structure. The work it provides is for women, however, and the potential migrant remains unemployed.

The second effect of weaving income is that it creates the potential for household accumulation and, in a dynamic sense, increases household incomes from other economic activities. In the case study villages, the typical means of investment are the purchase of land, agricultural machinery or means of transport, or the operation of a carpet workshop. Having two or more full-time weavers in the household is decisive in enabling accumulation in weaving households.

In Konya villages, where mono-crop mechanised agriculture is predominant, weaving income is typically earmarked to purchase cultivable land, which means that the plot is then given out to a share-cropper for cultivation. If prior to the purchase of land the household is landless, weaving income thus secures the subsistence crop, wheat, for the household. In households where subsistence production is already ensured through landholdings, the additional plot allows wheat to be produced as a cash crop. Some households purchase agricultural machinery that allows the male head of household to become a farmer, share-cropping land of others.

In both Konya and Isparta villages, women's weaving earnings have enabled the men of their households to become workshop operators. As noted in Chapter 2, intermediaries need cash to make regular wage payments and to be able to extend advances on wages, until they are reimbursed by urban merchants. The presence of a number of weavers in the household is an important source of cash for the workshop operator. He relies on the wages of the household weavers to make wage and rent payments, or to finance the construction of the workshop.

In the Döşemealtı and Niğde-2 villages, weaving incomes enable purchases of trucks for merchandise transport or minibuses for

passengers. In the Döşemealtı village, most households have access
to small plots where they engage in year-round vegetable farming
geared to the nearby metropolitan market. Partly because vegetables
grown for the market have raised land values considerably in recent
years, some men have instead used weaving earnings to purchase trucks.
The same spending pattern is observed in the Niğde-2 village as well,
but contrary to the Döşemealtı village, weaving income is not spent on
land due to its infertility rather than scarcity. In both villages,
men from two or three households join household resources to make the
down-payment for the purchase of a truck. The debt on the truck can
be paid within a few years, out of the earnings of women's continuous
weaving and men's lorry driving.

     In some of these households, through the purchase of means of
production, weaving income has lost its relative importance over time
and is no longer the primary source of household income, even if it
has been crucial at the initial stages of the household life cycle.
It is important to note, however, that through the process of accumulation fuelled by women's weaving men may change occupation and
class, while women have no property rights over the means of production purchased. In addition, weaving income may generate employment. The purchase of trucks or minibuses creates employment for
men or allows them to move out of farming. In regions where agriculture does not provide any paid or unpaid work for men, land
purchases transform men from landless unemployed to "landed" unemployed,
without generating pressures on them to start weaving or to seek
alternative employment. In these regions, women's weaving enhances
household incomes in both the immediate and dynamic sense, yet it
does not generate jobs.

Households headed by women

     The extended family structure, the low incidence of divorce and
the custom that young divorced or separated women return to their
natal households reduce the incidence of female-headed households
in the sample. None the less, according to the household composition
criteria stated in Chapter 2, 15 per cent of the sample weavers
belong to households that are headed by women, where either the
principal weaver or her mother is the household head. The summary
indicators presented in table 26 indicate that these households are
economically worse off than households headed by men. Hence,
findings of this study are consistent with recent evidence from
various parts of the Third World, that there is a higher incidence
of poverty among households headed by women (Youssef and Hetler,
1983).
     Table 26 shows that households headed by women are poorer, and
they own and cultivate substantially smaller plots. Slightly fewer
than half of these households are de facto headed by women due to the
temporary absence of adult men. The most common basis for de facto
female household headship is the recurrent seasonal migration of the

adult male in the household, which results from insufficient access
to land. Most of these migrants work in various construction and
service sector jobs in different parts of Turkey, and reside with
their families for less than six months of the year. The migrants
often do not make remittances to the rural household, however, largely
due to their low earnings relative to the cost of living in urban
areas. Even if remittances are sent, they are insufficient to support
the rural household and thus weaving becomes a major source of income
for these households. Similarly, in de jure female-headed households, divorced or widowed women often lose access to land and become
dependent on weaving income and financial assistance from their
parents or other relatives.

Table 26: Economic position of household by status of head of
household
(figures represent averages)

| | Status of head of household | | t-test[a] |
	Headed by woman (N=20)	Headed by man (N=113)	
Household income per adult (TL)	88 528	118 074	2.23 (0.0274)
Income per head (TL)	58 114	88 277	2.45 (0.0155)
Land in property[b] (hectares)	0.99 (N=10)	3.73 (N=89)	2.04 (0.0439)
Land in usufruct[c] (hectares)	0.52 (N=13)	3.46 (N=92)	2.49 (0.0143)
Agricultural income per adult (TL)	21 009	44 780	2.17 (0.0321)
Share of weaving in household income (%)	49	36	1.92 (0.0564)
Weaving income per weaver (TL)	63 654	82 332	1.45 (0.1507)
Number of household weavers	1.6	1.8	1.18 (0.2391)
Weaving output per weaver (knots)	921 444	1 271 855	1.69 (0.0943)

[a] Significance levels are reported in parentheses.

[b] Excludes landless households.

[c] Excludes households that do not have land in usufruct.

In per adult terms, average income from agricultural production of households headed by women is half that of households headed by men (table 26). Where they engage in agricultural production, the former are at a disadvantage. Those households headed by women that have access to land often cannot engage in the cultivation of cash crops. This is not so much due to their small holdings, but because of the shortage of family workers and lack of funds to purchase agricultural inputs. A shortage of family labour constrains the ability to draw on assistance from kin and neighbours through the exchange of labour to meet labour requirements during peak demand periods, and forces the household to rely on wage labour, which is often too costly for households headed by women. Likewise, due to shortage of funds households headed by women cannot purchase insecticides and fertilisers to increase yields.

Compared to households headed by men, the number of household weavers is not significantly lower in those headed by women but weaving income per weaver is substantially lower, although the difference is not statistically significant. The fact that the average weaving output of female-headed households is one-third less than the output of households headed by men can be attributed to the higher incidence of female-headed households in regions of home weaving in the sample. The lower rate of output associated with home weaving accounts for the lower carpet output. None the less, on average, weaving income constitutes half the household income in these households, indicating their dependence on weaving.

This discussion of the relative economic position of households headed by women shows that solely in terms of weaving income women in these households bear primary economic responsibility in supporting their households. Thus, the temporary or permanent absence of adult men indeed renders these households economically disadvantaged. If one is to adopt an alternative definition of household headship that is solely based on economic responsibility rather than the demographic criteria used so far, it is possible to identify households in which women are the "primary bread-winners".[7] According to this criterion and considering weaving activity alone, as noted earlier, in 26.3 per cent of sample households weaving income generated by all household weavers accounts for more than 50 per cent of household income. Measuring women's economic contribution in other activities besides weaving would certainly increase the proportion of weavers who are primary bread-winners in their household.

Conclusion

By focusing on the economic position of weaving households, this chapter has placed carpet-weaving employment within the broader framework of the agrarian structure, proletarianisation and rural-urban migration in Turkey. It has shown that weaving is linked with different agrarian structures, which affect the volume of weaving via both the demands placed by crop production on women's labour time and the adequacy of agricultural income in securing household subsistence. Average carpet output is substantially higher in villages of mono-crop agriculture, where women do not have competing work responsibilities in agriculture and households are dependent on non-agricultural sources of income. If the distribution of cultivable landholdings in Turkey is considered, weaving households have access to less land. Yet, weaving is not necessarily and solely associated with rural poverty and proletarianisation. In different rural contexts and given different household socio-economic and demographic characteristics, weaving income plays a range of roles, from preventing full-scale proletarianisation to enabling accumulation. This chapter has shown the crucial role of weaving income in the process of rural social differentiation, enabling men to change occupation in certain cases.

Notes

[1] Land in usufruct is calculated by adding up land in ownership, land rented in, land taken in to sharecrop, land lent by kin, share of land jointly cultivated, and subtracting from this sum land rented out and land given to share-croppers.

[2] Agricultural tasks reported in table 20 are defined on the basis of the most restricted definition of agricultural work — fieldwork for crop production — and hence underestimate women's overall participation in agricultural work. Recent studies on rural women insist on the adoption of a wider definition of agricultural work that includes tasks such as agricultural processing and animal production, which are predominantly women's work, in order to measure women's agricultural participation accurately (Deere and de Leal, 1982).

[3] The following wage work for men is available: threshing the grain (in all villages); preparing the soil for tobacco planting (Milas, Sındırgı); harvesting olives (Milas); pruning fruit trees, spading the soil of orchards and vineyards (Isparta, Niğde-1); reaping wheat with a sickle (Isparta, Döşemealtı, Milas, Sındırgı).

[4] In the calculation of household income, the value of subsistence production has been imputed using farm-gate prices. See Appendix II for a description of the calculation of household income in this study.

[5] A similar inverse relationship between weaving output and total household incomes from non-weaving sources is also observed. The impact of economic compulsion and agricultural work responsibilities on weaving output under the two agrarian structures are tested using multiple regression analysis in Berik (1986).

[6] The component of cash income is not easily separable from the monetised component because those households that engage in cash crop cultivation consume a portion of their output.

[7] Preference for the use of the term "primary bread-winner" rather than de facto (female) head of household is expressed in ILO: Rural women workers in Asia (Geneva, 1982).

CHAPTER 4

CARPET WEAVING AND WOMEN'S POSITION

This chapter examines the position of weavers as women and
evaluates the implications of the characteristics of weaving employment presented in Chapters 2 and 3 for the women's status and roles.
The cross-sectional nature of the study limits our evaluation of
the impact of participation in paid employment on the weaver's
position over time. Thus, the position of weavers is evaluated
across the sample in relation to demographic and employment characteristics, educational and economic variables. Having quantified and
illustrated the weavers' contribution to household income in
Chapter 3, this chapter specifically considers whether the autonomy
of weavers depends on the extent of their contribution to household
income. The major part focuses on women's control over their labour
power, product and income, and their ability to participate in making
purchases. The last two sections of the chapter examine women's
perceptions of their work alternatives and working conditions, as
well as their perceptions of prospects for change, given the
limited choices.

Control over labour power

For most weavers, the decision to weave is not an individual
decision, especially because they start weaving in childhood. Whether
the young girl just out of elementary school starts weaving or not is
determined by village traditions. In fact, her life choices are
determined at birth. In Konya villages, the birth of a daughter is
celebrated by the father as "It's a factory!", rather than "It's a
girl!". This exclamation aptly captures the position of women in a
community where they have become income-generating assets.

The prospective "income stream" resulting from the daughter's
labour has a detrimental effect on her schooling prospects, even in
the context of increasing availability of schools in rural areas.
While educational opportunities in rural areas are expanding, young
women have less access to schooling compared to young men. As pointed
out in Chapter 2, there seem to have been some changes in attitudes
between generations with respect to educating women. A larger proportion of the younger weavers have completed five years of elementary
school than their older counterparts. However, even in places where

69

the junior high school is located in the village the number of girls allowed to continue beyond elementary school is disproportionately low. The prospective income stream helps reproduce the widespread attitude that schooling is unnecessary and even an embarrassment for women.

Besides the fact that the weaver's life choices are determined at birth, at later stages in her life the prevalence of gossip and criticism act as mechanisms of social control which ensure that the weaver does not consider alternatives to weaving. The prestige of being a dutiful and obedient daughter, daughter-in-law and wife often acts as a reward in maintaining the continuity of weaving. The fact that weaving may be combined relatively easily with other responsibilities of the weaver and is very closely associated with gender identity means that it is considered almost embarrassing not to weave, regardless of the household's economic position. Thus, when the 16-year old daughter of a wealthy landowner (who owns both a tractor and a combine harvester) in the Konya-1 village is asked why she weaves, she replies that her father wants her to. "My father says, 'If you don't weave, what will you do idle at home, when all the women your age are weaving?'". Since she was denied an education beyond elementary school and does not have any other alternatives for employment, what will she indeed do? She works under exactly the same working conditions as other weavers. Unlike most workshop weavers, however, she has more control over decisions pertaining to weaving. She was permitted to attend the sewing-embroidery course in the village, sponsored by the State, which lasted for six months during 1983. While taking this course, she worked on "pocket money carpets" only, keeping her earnings, despite the fact that she is indebted to an intermediary for the wage advances her father obtained to meet the wedding-related expenses of her sister.

A seasonal wage worker in the Niğde-1 village, who is more dependent on his wife's weaving than the landowner is on his daughter's weaving income, expressed the reason for his wife's weaving in the following manner: "If she does not weave, she will idle and gossip. Weaving keeps the woman at home and prevents her from indulging in gossip". Ironically, it is women who are in danger of idling; men do not idle.

Weaving in a workshop is associated with diminished control of weavers over their labour power. To the extent that, contrary to home weaving, a wider range of decisions arise in workshop weaving, and that weavers themselves have little or no say in making these decisions, it is possible to argue that the expansion of workshop weaving decreases women's control over their labour power.

The alliance between the workshop owner and the weaver's male relative has implications for earnings, working conditions and the weaver's autonomy. Firstly, as discussed in Chapter 2, the alliance ensures a continued supply of weaving labour for the intermediary's workshop. In the workshop, the pace of weaving is maintained and intensified through various social practices, if not overt pressures from senior household members. Given that by custom the oldest male has the greatest decision-making power in the family, he exercises his power in various decisions related to weaving work, as revealed by the weaving histories of workshop weavers: the choice of the workshop the weaver is to work at; when and whether or not she is to interrupt, stop or resume weaving after an interruption. Senior women in the family act as "supervisors" in implementing these decisions.

Weaving at home, the weaver maintains control over the allocation of tasks during the working day, and there is less room for pressures to increase the pace of weaving. Beyond differences in the labour process, however, there is variation in the extent to which women exercise control over decisions related to weaving work. Among home weavers of similar age group, for example, Döşemealtı, Sındırgı and Milas weavers appear to have greater autonomy in these decisions than Afyon weavers. The difference can be attributed to varying structural and economic conditions. While all four villages are integrated into the commodity market through the sale of cash crops, the former three have a more flexible sexual division of labour in agricultural tasks, while in the Afyon village men engage in fewer agricultural tasks. Similarly, differences in conditions of work in workshops between Isparta and Konya regions may be shaped by differences in the avail- ability of income-earning alternatives and the sexual division of labour. A more rigid sexual division of labour and a narrower range of economic alternatives in the Konya region sustain more rigid work schedules, and are associated with greater control over women. In the Isparta region, on the other hand, a more flexible division of labour in agriculture and a wider range of economic alternatives are associated with less pressure on weavers. Moreover, whether or not men engage in weaving seems to depend on the flexi- bility of the sexual division of labour in activities other than weaving. The small number of male weavers who weave along with sample weavers are from tobacco-growing Milas and Sındırgı villages, where there is greater overlap in the agricultural fieldwork that men and women perform.

Control over product and income, and participation in purchases

In rural Turkey, adult women have very limited control over income. Summarising the results of the Hacettepe University Surveys of 1968 and 1973, Özbay (1985) notes that despite some change towards greater participation in decision-making in the household, women's participation in decisions is low. Among four categories of decision- makers (husband, wife, husband and wife, older members of the family), in 1973 the proportion of households in which spending decisions were made either by older family members or by the husband ranged from 63.6 per cent (in deciding how much to spend on food) to 79.7 per cent (in deciding how to spend family income).

Table 27 shows how weavers fare on various aspects of income control, handling cash, and participation in marketing carpets and making purchases. Only 23.3 per cent of independent weavers participate in the sale of carpets they have produced. These weavers are either currently married, divorced or widowed, and their average age is 41, as opposed to 26 for those who are not involved in the sale of carpets. Most of these weavers are from the Niğde-1 village, where it is socially acceptable for older women to sell carpets in the weekly market of the nearby town.

Table 27: Weavers' control over product and income, and participation in purchases
(percentages)

	Yes		No
Participates in selling carpet (N=73)	23.3		76.7
Receives own earnings (N=127)	29.9		70.1
Keeps cash (N=129)	55.8		44.2
Has input into decisions over spending weaving income (N=130)	74.6		25.4
	Considerable	Some	None
Has input into decisions over spending household income (N=132)	28.8	27.3	43.9
	Yes		No
Participates in making purchases (N=130)	72.3		27.7

With respect to income control, the general pattern that emerges from this study is that it is the male head of household who receives income, keeps cash, makes spending decisions and carries out monetary transactions. Seventy per cent of weavers do not receive their earnings themselves. Only 21.3 per cent of independent weavers, 31.3 per cent of outworkers and 47.2 per cent of workshop weavers receive any part of their earnings themselves. If wages are paid outside the home, then the male kin of outworkers receive the payments. The proportion of workshop weavers that receive at least a part of their earnings is higher as a result of two practices: Isparta weavers are usually paid their weekly wages directly and Konya weavers are permitted to receive about one-sixth of their annual weaving earnings. The latter is the "pocket money" portion of the weaver's annual income that results from weaving during the breaks taken in between carpets.

Fifty-six per cent of sample weavers have access to cash, but only 38.3 per cent hold cash for personal or household expenditures (rather than simply for incidental small expenses). It is generally socially acceptable for widows or weavers whose husbands are seasonally or frequently away at work to keep their income and oversee its spending. Where weavers live in an extended family household, even headship of the nuclear family does not guarantee that the weaver will keep cash (or decide on its spending), since there are other men in the household.

Twenty-eight per cent of weavers do not go shopping at all. Whether or not the weaver goes shopping is an indicator of the weaver's physical mobility and contact with the world outside her home or workshop, i.e. her level of interaction with the "public sphere", as well as a reflection of her participation in spending.

With respect to spending, a spectrum of behavioural patterns is observed in different regions. While in some villages married women spend their incomes, sometimes alone, in others weavers do not have the chance to spend their income, not even together with their husbands or when personal items are to be bought. The mobility of unmarried weavers in terms of actual spending is on the whole more restricted. While in some villages unmarried weavers accompany their parents in shopping for personal items, in others they are not allowed to go shopping under any circumstances.

Weavers whose husbands are permanently or temporarily absent generally have more freedom to go shopping. For younger women in such circumstances, however, dependence on male kin for purchases is more likely. According to the small trader husband of a weaver from a village in the Niğde region (not a case study village), his being away for eight months of the year was not a sufficient reason for his 31-year-old wife to go shopping in the weekly market of the nearby town. He expressed his disapproval of his wife's going shopping in no ambiguous terms: "If I hear that she has gone shopping in the bazaar in my absence, I'll come back and break her legs". This weekly market is the same market where the independent weavers of the Niğde-1 village sell the carpets they have produced. This illustrates that there is variation in socially acceptable patterns of behaviour for women, not only by age, but also by village. It also suggests that the threat of violence is effective in ensuring women's compliance with cultural patterns, an opinion also expressed by a landless seasonal construction worker in the Afyon village: "You have to beat women once in a while to keep them in line".

Socialisation in restricted physical mobility begins at an early age. The husband of a weaver in the Afyon village opposes his 3-year-old daughter from going to the grocer's store close to their home to purchase candy. He does not want the child to acquire a sense of freedom in making purchases. Restricted physical mobility does not apply to all activities outside the home, however. Born to a landless household, when she grows up this child will most probably have to work in the fields for a wage, along with weaving three months in the winter, just as her older sisters do today.

It is difficult to study the dynamics of actual decision-making within the family with respect to spending. This is partly due to the completely private nature of the exercise of influence in the family, and partly because in general no household member is regarded as making decisions as an autonomous individual, although it is socially recognised that senior and male members have greater authority in the family than other members. Thus, probing into who makes decisions in the household through direct questions during interviews did not seem likely to produce accurate answers. Consequently, in order to capture the realm of decision-making as well as limit the number of structured questions in the questionnaire, open-ended questions and the impressions obtained during interviews were used in evaluating weavers' influence on spending decisions. Specifically, two variables were identified and evaluated: whether or not the weaver has any influence on decisions on spending her weaving income and the extent of influence the weaver has on household spending decisions in general.[1]

Weavers seem to have limited say in household spending decisions: 25.4 per cent had no input into decisions over spending their weaving income, while 44 per cent had no input into household spending decisions in general. As the list of items on which weaving income is spent indicates (see Chapter 3), some purchases directly benefit weavers. Part of the weaving income of the young unmarried weaver is spent on her dowry, or a dowry is prepared for her in the future in return for her current weaving labour. The size and content of the dowry depends on the household's economic position, and also varies by region. Some young weavers complained that they had no say in how their earnings were spent and expressed either hope or doubt that their weaving might ensure a better dowry for them in the future. Aside from dowry spending, which constitutes the main personal spending item that women weavers have claim to, weavers also benefit from purchases of various consumer durables that reduce their daily workload. To give a striking example, the refrigerator bought by lump-sum wage advances in the Konya-1 village reduces the need for daily cooking, and hence the conflict between women's domestic responsibilities and workshop weaving, thus ensuring that the weaver devotes more time to weaving.

Other difficulties in studying income control pertain to assessing the relative position of weavers in comparison to non-weaver women and over time. Since the study design did not include a non-weaver reference group, the former comparison was not attempted. Yet such a comparison did not seem feasible because all women within a particular age group, which is considered as the weaving age group in each village, are weavers. The difficulties in comparing the present position of weavers relative to their position when they started weaving, on the other hand, stem from the cross-sectional nature of the study as well as from the fact that weavers start weaving in childhood. It is difficult to detect whether or not participation in weaving has any impact on income control, because

in most cases the effect of contribution to household earnings
cannot be separated from that of growing older and of a change in
marital status. In Döşemealtı and Sındırgı villages, where carpet
weaving was recently introduced and the average age at which
weavers began weaving is higher, group interviews revealed that,
compared to the pre-weaving period, women have more say in decisions
over spending weaving income as well as total household income in
general. Even in these cases, it is difficult to disentangle the
effect of growing older from that of participation in weaving
activity.

In order to examine the relationship between income control
and various economic and personal characteristics of weavers, a
composite index was constructed. This index, termed the "financial
autonomy index", takes on values between 0 (representing no financial
autonomy), and 1 (representing complete financial autonomy) and is
based on four variables that capture dimensions of income control and
handling cash: (a) whether or not the weaver receives her weaving
earnings herself; (b) whether or not the weaver keeps cash at all;
(c) whether or not the weaver has influence on spending decisions
over weaving income; and (d) the extent to which the weaver has an
influence on household spending decisions, in general.[2] The
frequency distributions of these variables are given in table 27.

The distribution of index values in table 28 shows that 19
per cent of sample weavers have a score of 0, while 13.2 per cent
have a score of 1 or "complete" financial autonomy, with 50 per cent
of weavers having a score of 0.70 and above. Table 29 presents the
relationship between the financial autonomy index and weaving income
across the case study villages. The average index values arranged
in descending order in the first column of table 29 reveal a range
from a high of 0.66 in Döşemealtı to a low of 0.35 in Afyon. A
cursory look at table 29 does not indicate a systematic relationship between the financial autonomy index and either measure of
weavers' income contribution. While the Afyon village ranks eighth
on all three variables, taking the villages as a whole, greater
financial autonomy is not associated with either higher or lower
values of weaving income contribution.

The financial autonomy index is also used to explore the
relationship of autonomy pertaining to income control to various
characteristics of weavers and their households: the age of the
weaver; years of schooling she has completed; the type of household she lives in; headship status of her household; her annual
weaving income and its share in total household income; and total
income of her household expressed in per adult terms. Given the
traditional pattern that women gain status with advancing age,
age is expected to be positively related to financial autonomy.
Living in an extended family household is expected to be associated
with a lower financial autonomy, since the weaver is in a lower
position in the age and gender hierarchies in this type of household. Relative to women weavers in households headed by men,
those in households headed by women are expected to participate
more in decisions pertaining to spending. The number of years of

schooling is expected to be positively correlated with financial autonomy, because education might break the traditional pattern whereby women gain status. Weaving in a workshop is expected to be associated with higher financial autonomy, because it is paid work done outside the home. The magnitudes of household income, weaving income, and the share of weaving income in total household income are each expected to be positively associated with financial autonomy.

Table 28: Distribution of the financial autonomy index values

Index value	N	%
0.00	23	19.0
0.15	8	6.6
0.30	1	0.8
0.40	2	1.7
0.55	26	21.5
0.70	31	25.6
0.85	14	11.6
1.00	16	13.2
Total	121	100.0

The relationship of the financial autonomy index to each of these variables is reported in table 30. The absolute magnitude or relative importance of weaving income do not have a significant consistent effect on financial autonomy. Neither does total household income expressed in per adult terms have a systematic relationship to the index, suggesting that financial autonomy is relatively insensitive to household economic position. Instead, there is a strong positive association between financial autonomy and the age of the weaver, which reflects the weaver's position in the family hierarchy. The financial autonomy of weavers who belong to extended family households tends to be substantially lower than that of weavers in nuclear family households. This once again reflects the lower position of the weaver in the family hierarchy. Those weavers who live in households headed by women, even if the head is the weaver's mother, have greater financial autonomy. There is no statistically significant relationship between financial autonomy and weaving labour process, and level of education does not bear a systematic relationship to financial autonomy.[3]

These results suggest that the financial autonomy of weavers is primarily shaped by the weaver's position in the family hierarchy and is not sensitive to economic variables. The fact that the relative importance of weaving income and its absolute magnitude do not have statistically significant effects on the financial autonomy of weavers indicates that greater financial autonomy is not the outcome of participation in paid work, but is primarily governed by factors that operate irrespective of weavers' participation in paid work in carpet weaving.

Table 29: Financial autonomy index values and absolute and relative contributions of principal weavers by case study village (figures represent averages) (N=121)

Village	Financial autonomy index	Weaving income (TL)	Relative contribution[a]
Döşemealtı	0.662	90 758 (3)[b]	0.226 (6)[b]
Niğde-1	0.656	30 074 (7)	0.173 (7)
Isparta-1,2	0.637	85 256 (4)	0.256 (4)
Milas	0.608	55 682 (6)	0.229 (5)
Sındırgı	0.592	114 524 (2)	0.370 (2)
Konya-1,2	0.431	143 834 (1)	0.323 (3)
Niğde-2	0.430	81 478 (5)	0.418 (1)
Afyon	0.350	18 244 (8)	0.065 (8)
F-statistic	2.03	20.77	4.59
Significance level	0.0573	0.0000	0.0002

[a] Share of principal weaver's weaving income in total household income.

[b] Numbers in parentheses indicate position if variable values were arranged in descending order.

Table 30: Relationship of financial autonomy index to various
characteristics of the principal weaver and her household,
and to characteristics of weaving employment
(figures represent averages)

	N^a	Financial autonomy index	F-test[b]
Weaver's age in years			
15-20	48	0.39	10.79
21-30	39	0.61	(0.0000)
31-40	24	0.61	
41-66	10	0.93	
Years of schooling			
None	33	0.63	2.16
Less than 5 years	6	0.28	(0.0960)
5 years	76	0.53	
More than 5 years	6	0.56	
Type of household			
Nuclear family	102	0.58	6.68
Extended family	19	0.37	(0.0110)
Household headship status			
Headed by a man	102	0.51	7.15
Headed by a woman	19	0.73	(0.0086)
Weaving labour process			
Home	85	0.56	0.78
Workshop	36	0.51	(0.3781)
Annual net weaving income of the principal weaver (TL)			
6,500-36,500	31	0.52	3.84
36,600-73,000	31	0.71	(0.0116)
73,500-126,000	30	0.45	
127,000-226,600	29	0.51	
Share of principal weaver's weaving income in household income (%)			
1-25	76	0.53	1.271
26-50	34	0.56	(0.2876)
51-75	5	0.82	
75-100	6	0.51	

Table 30 (continued)

	N[a]	Financial autonomy index	F-test[b]
Per adult household income (TL)			
16,800-71,800	30	0.56	2.01
73,400-107,200	31	0.44	(0.1167)
108,800-145,800	30	0.55	
146,200-340,100	30	0.64	

[a] N=121.

[b] Significance levels are reported in parentheses.

Weavers' work alternatives and preferences

As discussed earlier, sample weavers have very few alternatives for paid work. Yet when questioned, the majority of weavers claimed they would like to have worked at another income-generating activity rather than weave. The kind of activity for which the weavers expressed a preference over carpet weaving is salaried work or non-agricultural wage employment outside the home, mainly because of the perceived income security associated with such jobs. The over-whelming majority of both home and workshop weavers identified agri-cultural work as inferior to carpet weaving, regardless of whether or not this alternative actually exists in their village. Weavers prefer weaving to agricultural work mainly because weaving is done indoors ("away from the heat and cold").

Slightly over half the sample weavers prefer workshop weaving. Regardless of marital status, the number and age of their children, all workshop weavers prefer weaving in the workshop as opposed to weaving at home, and some home weavers also prefer workshop weaving. Since the majority of weavers do not have a choice between the two labour processes, the expressed preference is not based on an appraisal of the characteristics of both labour processes but on scanty information at best. Preference for a particular labour process is strongly influenced by the current weaving practice (table 31), the familiarity with and availability of an alternative labour process in the village (table 32), and the availability of assistance from non-weaver women in the household (table 33).

In general, workers' preferences for home weaving reflect the considerations in combining weaving work with reproductive responsi-bilities. Most value the flexibility that weaving at home allows in carrying out household chores. Where currently there is no work-shop weaving, single women also expressed a preference for home weaving, for fear of the possible gossip if they were to weave in a workshop.

79

Those weavers who prefer workshop weaving state that it is more enjoyable to weave in a workshop and that it is possible to earn more relative to weaving at home. Some workshop weavers enjoy socialising with others in the workshop, while others enjoy the relative freedom of being out of the home, away from the close supervision of senior women in the household. Workshop weavers are unanimous that it would not be possible to maintain as high a rate of output if they were to weave at home. Weavers with young children complained of interruptions caused by their children and the children's damage to the carpet when they wove at home.

Few independent weavers think their unit earnings would be lower if they were to work in the workshop. Although independent weavers and workshop weavers did not actually compare unit earnings and rate of output, interestingly enough, their speculation matches the findings of this study: unit earnings of independent weavers are higher than those of both the putting-out system and workshop weavers; and workshop weavers earn more as a whole due to the higher rate of output in workshops.

Table 31: Preference for labour process by current location

Preference	Current location			
	Home		Workshop	
	N	%	N	%
Home	48	75	-	-
Workshop	16	25	38	100
Total	64	100.0	38	100.0

Chi-square: 50.87
Significance: 0.0000

Table 32: Preference for labour process by familiarity with workshop weaving

Preference	Familiarity with workshop weaving					
	There has never been workshop weaving in the village		At one time there existed workshop weaving		Currently workshop weaving exists	
	N	%	N	%	N	%
Home	24	77.4	21	75.0	3	7.0
Workshop	7	22.6	7	25.0	40	93.0
Total	31	100.0	28	100.0	43	100.0

Chi-square: 47.97
Significance: 0.0000

Table 33: Preference for labour process by availability of
assistance in the household

Preference	No. of non-weaver women in household					
	0		1		2	
	N	%	N	%	N	%
Home	32	69.6	13	29.5	3	25
Workshop	14	30.4	31	70.5	9	75
Total	46	100.0	44	100.0	12	100

Chi-square: 17.11
Significance: 0.0002

Weavers' perceptions of working conditions and prospects for change

In general, workshop weavers' perceptions of weaving varied
with the stage in the weaver's life cycle as well as by region. In
Konya workshops, young weavers complained of the pressures to weave.
Some even refused to take advantage of the "pocket money carpet"
option. Most weavers stated their unhappiness about having to
conform to the established daily weaving schedules, particularly in
summer months. When weaving days are long, the weavers still have
to attend to some household chores after the weaving day, and the
fact that they have to start weaving at dawn does not excuse them
from staying up as late as other household members. While men can
sleep late, women have to adjust to much shorter sleeping hours.
On the other hand, some workshop weavers with young children stated
that they are content with the present division of labour in the
household, where their mother-in-law takes care of the children or
attends to household animals.

As compared to Konya weavers, weavers in Isparta workshops
appeared to have more harmonious relationships among themselves.
For them workshop weaving represented more freedom. This can be
attributed to the narrower age range of weavers, and lesser supervision by kin built into the daily operation of workshops in the
Isparta region.

In both regions, the physical condition of workshops vary.
Most are dark and cramped, and some are damp. Most weavers do not
complain about the poor condition of the workshops. Attempts to
maximise weaving earnings by both the intermediary and the weaver's
kin lead to total disregard for the condition of the workshop.
Poor lighting results in early deterioration of eyesight. Lengthy
hours of seated work on low benches from early childhood onwards
leads to deformities of the back. Shearing with heavy scissors
results in hand deformities in weavers who began weaving in early
childhood. Neither deformity was widespread, however, and neither

seemed to be associated solely with workshop weaving, but with the early age at which the weaver began weaving. Konya weavers also reported difficulties during childbirth, which they attributed to long hours of seated work.

In Konya workshops, where the weaving tenure of women is an uninterrupted 20 to 25 years, weavers are eager to be covered by the social security system, but are helpless against the allied opposition of their fathers, fathers-in-law or husbands with the intermediaries and merchants. Some were outspoken in complaining about the lack of coverage, although questions pertaining to social security could not be directly asked in the workshop setting. Given the limited chances of taking advantage of free state health services in rural areas, the main advantage the social security system has to offer to the rural weaver is retirement benefits. The intermediaries claim that coverage may be too costly for the merchants and may lead to the eventual loss of weaving employment in the village. Fathers oppose coverage in part due to this threat and in part because, according to the weavers, it is their daughters' future husbands who are to benefit from the deductions of today. They prefer a higher income stream today than to ensure their children's continued future earnings. By the time the weaver reaches adulthood and gets married, social security premiums are no longer worth paying, given that the weaver has already spent half her anticipated weaving tenure outside the coverage of the system. The problem is compounded by the fact that under the present law coverage cannot begin before the age of 16, which means that five years of the weaving tenure of most workers cannot be covered by the system. For home weavers, coverage is not even possible. According to the social security system, their weaving is not recognised as work.

Women recognise that through their work the household consumption level is maintained or expanded, yet they are generally fatalistic in their appraisal of their unequal workload and the unequal benefits they derive from their participation in weaving and their contribution to family income. As one Konya-2 weaver said: "We (women) take on these bums (economically inactive men), and support them". Most have internalised the consequences of their subordinate position in the gender and age hierarchies of the family, rarely question their situation and are generally pessimistic about prospects for change during their lifetime. A few pregnant weavers stated that they do not wish to have a daughter because of the prospects in life awaiting the child. Some Niğde-1 weavers, who have a daughter, said they did not wish her to weave carpets in the future but to get an education. Some added that their daughter would have to weave in any case because "it is the village custom".

The strength of traditional norms that govern women's position has an important influence on possibilities for change, since traditionally it is the age hierarchy among women that reinforces their unequal position. Since women gain status with age, older women usually act to preserve their position and therefore help reproduce the existing order of sexual inequality in the household.

Similarly, the prospect of future power and prestige, through the domination of younger women in the household, acts as an incentive for conformity in a system where women's alternatives are severely constrained.

Young weavers see the possibility for change in their position in marrying out of the village to a man from a non-weaving village or region. Others see the elimination of carpet weaving as women's work as the only solution towards improving their position. Konya-1 workshop weavers had no qualms about asking a rare visitor: "Go and tell Kenan Evren to outlaw carpet weaving"[4], a request that encapsulates their frustration with the atmosphere of compulsion in workshops, as well as the deeply ingrained belief that any change can only be spearheaded by the State. Yet others say: "If only this carpet were not exported ..." (so that there would be no demand for their work). Following the complaint, most add that they do not know how their families would subsist, if it were not for carpet weaving.

Conclusion

The foregoing discussion of the various factors that shape the decision-making power of rural carpet weavers indicates that, in general, weavers lack control over their labour power and their product, have limited control over income, and are restricted in making purchases. Variations in indicators of decision-making power with respect to weaving work, income control and participation in the market as sellers or buyers of commodities are related to age, marital status, household headship status and type of family structure, rather than to the extent of contribution to household income or household economic position. Moreover, weaving in a workshop intensifies the lack of female autonomy with respect to decisions affecting weaving employment. Workshop weavers are frustrated with working conditions and see the only possibility for improvement in their position in being relieved of weaving work. Yet, given the more social environment workshops offer and the lack of both work alternatives and access to schooling beyond elementary school, most weavers prefer weaving in a workshop rather than at home. The majority of weavers prefer weaving over agricultural fieldwork, although a salaried job, which is unattainable for almost all weavers, is clearly more desirable than weaving.

Notes

[1] Direct questions on these two variables were used in the pre-test questionnaire but were dropped in favour of an indirect approach for the reasons noted above.

[2] The weighting used in the construction of the index is as follows: receiving earnings and keeping cash have been given equal (0.15 each) but lower weights relative to the variables of influence on decisions over spending. Influence on decisions over spending weaving income and household spending decisions were weighted by 0.4 and 0.3, respectively. Greater weights were attached to the decision-making variables because these were considered to be more important in capturing "real control" relative to the more formal dimensions of control captured by the first two variables.

[3] Some of these results are modified when the effect of these variables (excluding household income level) on the financial autonomy index are explored in a multiple regression framework (Berik, 1986). Multiple regression analysis results indicate weaver's age and type of household structure to be the most important variables explaining variations in financial autonomy of weavers, while economic contribution has no effect on financial autonomy, thus confirming the results of bivariate analysis reported in table 30. The results pertaining to the relationship of financial autonomy to weaving labour process, household headship status and years of schooling are modified: financial autonomy of workshop weavers is significantly higher than that of home weavers, and household headship status does not have a statistically significant effect, while years of schooling have a slight positive effect on financial autonomy.

[4] Then the head of the ruling military National Security Council, and subsequently President of Turkey.

CHAPTER 5

CONCLUSION

Summary of findings

In this final chapter, we summarise the main findings of this study and discuss the possibilities for policy intervention to improve the conditions of work and socio-economic position of carpet weavers. The main objectives of this study were to make the carpet weavers in rural Turkey visible, to demonstrate the qualitative and quantitative significance of this work and to evaluate the position of weavers as women. The study has attempted to capture patterns in the carpet weavers' economic and social position across regions and diverse productive structures in both weaving and agriculture. Precisely due to the scope and exploratory nature of this study, however, caution should be exercised in making generalisations as a result. Thus, the findings summarised below should be regarded as tentative, requiring confirmation by further studies.

In its current form, carpet weaving is an activity based on women's subordinate position in the household and the dependence of poor and landless households on weaving income. Merchants and exporters take advantage of these features of the rural weaving labour force. The undervaluation of women's work on the grounds that the work is performed during "leisure" hours, or is performed while seated, weakens demands for higher pay for the skilled labour these women perform. None of the sample weavers has access to social benefits, despite the fact that a considerable proportion have been weaving for over 20 years (the length of time required for retirement of women under the SSL). Moreover, where they work in workshops, most weave in unhealthy conditions.

The study has shown how the weaver's contribution to household income is determined by the relation of production in weaving, house-hold composition and the prevailing agrarian and social structure. The weaving activity of principal weavers was found to account for 26 per cent of annual household earnings on average, while the proportional contribution of household weavers as a whole constituted 38 per cent of household income. The findings of the study with respect to the hypotheses outlined in the introduction are summar-ised in the paragraphs that follow.

1. The agrarian structure affects the volume of weaving in
two ways:
(a) The type of crops cultivated and the extent of mechanisation of
     agriculture affect the volume of weaving via the demands on
     women's labour time. The greater the agricultural work respons-
     ibilities of women, the less the time devoted to carpet weaving.
     In mono-culture, capital-intensive grain agriculture, there is
     no demand for women's labour as paid or unpaid workers, and
     this allows women to devote a greater amount of time to weaving.
     Labour-intensive crops produced under smallholder multi-crop
     agriculture, on the other hand, demand substantial time of
     women, and hence account for a lower carpet output.
(b) Household access to means of production and the magnitude of
     incomes from agriculture (or non-weaving sources) vary inversely
     with the volume of weaving. Women from both landed and landless
     households weave, but the greater the magnitude of earnings
     from alternative income sources, the lower the rate of weaving.
     Thus, acute landlessness and lower average incomes from agri-
     culture is another factor that accounts for greater average
     output of women from villages of mono-crop agriculture.
     Moreover, the relative contributions of both individual and
     household weavers as a whole are highest in the poorest house-
     holds, reaching 42 per cent and 49 per cent, respectively.
2. Reproductive responsibilities of weavers do not conflict
with weaving. Home weaving is compatible with child care and the
performance of domestic tasks, often through stretching the length
of the working day. Workshop weaving is rendered compatible with
the reproductive responsibilities of women through task specialisation among women in the household or the extension of assistance
from female kin who are not household members. The study has found
that, in general, having young children does not have a negative
effect on weaving output.
3. Workshop weaving generates a higher volume of weaving than
home weaving because of the greater continuity of weaving and higher
intensity of work in workshops. The study has demonstrated that
women's subordinate position in the gender and age hierarchies of
the household is built into the daily operation of workshops and is
effective in maintaining the greater productivity of workshop
weavers.
4. Given the variations in the economic standing of weaving
households, carpet weaving not only counters proletarianisation and
pauperisation of rural households, but also contributes to household accumulation. In some households (for example, female-headed
households), income from weaving is crucial for basic subsistence,
while in others it makes the purchase of durable consumption and
investment goods possible. The greater overall magnitude of weaving
income and the lump-sum receipt of weaving earnings are crucial in
making accumulation possible. Hence, underlying the possibility of
accumulation is the number of women in the household.
5. The study shows that the effects of women's participation
in paid work on their status and roles are uneven. The increasing

value of women as cash generators, especially when combined with limited economic alternatives for the household, inhibits the life choices of women. Educational opportunities are stifled. The discussion pertaining to women's control over decisions concerning weaving employment indicates the limited autonomy of weavers. In this respect, workshop weavers have the least autonomy. While home weavers control the pace of their work and make decisions at least over the allocation of their time among tasks, workshop weavers have no such flexibility. The extension of patriarchal control to the workplace not only maintains and extends the pace and volume of weaving, but also implies the weakening of female autonomy in decisions with respect to wage work. On the other hand, the study also finds that this diminished autonomy over employment decisions is accompanied by a trend to allow women some control over their earnings, even if as a way to ensure greater productivity in work-shops.

6. The study shows that the importance of women's economic contribution to their households, which is so often regarded as the key lever whereby participation in paid work is likely to effect changes towards gender equality, does not account for greater decision-making power. Greater (quantitative) importance of weaving income does not lead to greater financial autonomy, as measured by a composite index constructed on the basis of four variables of income control and cash handling. Instead, financial autonomy is governed by variables that capture women's position in the age and gender hierarchies of the household. Thus, the cultural patterns that shape women's position in rural Turkey (women bear the heaviest work-load and have the least autonomy when they are young) appear to be unaffected by participation in paid work in carpet weaving.

*   *   *

The relative insensitivity of women's subordinate position to economic variables should come as no surprise. The discussion of social relations in carpet weaving and the nature of the activity explains why women's autonomy is insensitive to the importance of their economic contribution. In rural Turkish society, carpet weaving is compatible with traditional female roles and is socially acceptable as women's work in terms of limited physical mobility outside the home. This study shows that weaving both in the home and at workshops in small rural communities do not challenge existing gender relations and the ideology embedded in the daily social practices, and therefore do not confer power on women. In general, the conditions under which weavers engage in paid work both depend on and reproduce their subordinate position as women. Weaving is closely intertwined with the existing gender relations in each community and where it was recently introduced, the activity has adapted to the cultural patterns in each region. Even where workshop weaving is predominant, engaging in weaving does not introduce contradictions that would set off changes in other areas of decision-making in the household. In fact, workshop weaving appears to be part of the problem and not the solution to the lack of decision-making power of women. Precisely because of the continuity between familial relations and the social relations in paid work, participation in carpet weaving or weavers' greater economic contribution is not a sufficient condition for change towards gender equality. Thus, the study shows that the effects of paid work on women's position are shaped by pre-existing relations between the sexes and the degree of women's subordination in each community, as well as relations in paid work.

However, it is also important to recognise the material basis of the cultural and ideological context of pre-existing gender relations. Across villages there is some variation in aspects of women's position that could be related to structural and economic differences. The comparison of two regions of workshop weaving, for example, suggests that when women engage in an income-generating activity (as compatible as weaving is with the tradi-tional roles of women) in the context of lack of income alter-natives and a rigid sexual division of labour, this leads to greater male control over women's labour power. This indicates that the effects of participation in paid work on women's position are more likely to be positive when the relations between women and men are relatively more equal in the first place.

While this study has not quantified the relative workload of men and women, field observations reveal severe inequalities in the work burden, even if only weaving activity is taken into account. The fact that women weave does not lessen their non-weaving workload. Women continue bearing other productive work responsibilities in addition to all the reproductive tasks, upon all of which weaving is superimposed, thereby creating year-round work for women. This inequality is even more pronounced where mechanised mono-crop farming is predominant.

Policy recommendations

Four areas of concern for policy-makers emerge from this study: (a) earnings for skilled weaving labour that are at or below the minimum wage; (b) lack of social benefits for these invisible weavers, most of whom weave for a lifetime; (c) poor physical condition of workshops; (d) lack of control of actual producers over their labour power and the products of their labour. Measures must be taken towards the improvement of working con-ditions, the provision of social benefits, increased earnings and the creation of means to confer power on the actual producers.

The first step in this direction must be the official recog-nition of carpet weaving as "work". This must be accompanied by a fundamental change in the present policy approach towards carpet weaving. As pointed out in Chapter 1, the current outlook has as its sole objective the expansion of production and exports.

Concerns voiced by merchants, co-operative administrators and, with few exceptions, civil servants, centre on obstacles and conditions favourable to the expansion of carpet production, while co-operative officials take pride in how fast carpets are completed in their village.

This study has shown, however, that the objective of maximising output is incompatible with the improvement of women's working and living conditions. Maximising carpet output implies maximising not only weaving income but also women's work effort, which leads to an intensified pace of weaving and lengthy hours of seated work. As household incomes increase, women benefit from having a refrigerator or a better roof. However, the existing inequality in the distribution of the fruits of women's labour between men and women prevents women weavers from benefiting directly from increased work effort.

Changes in policy must be accompanied by concrete measures to tackle all four problems stated above. If these problems are to be confronted with the expectation of a reasonable measure of success, then fundamental changes in the organisation of production and marketing of carpets have to be undertaken, and efforts must be made to come to terms with the social and ideological context. A new type of collective organisation based on direct participation of weavers should be established. The institutional structure of such a collective organisation must be different from the existing organisational forms, be sensitive to gender concerns and not be built on the assumption of an identity of interests between "the head of household" and the weaver.

At present, there are no formal or informal organisations among women carpet weavers. One-fifth of the weavers work for weaving co-operatives, either where the co-operative is a non-profit intermediary to Sümerbank or where it owns the means of production and extends them to workshop owners, who organise production. In addition, until the late 1970s most of the independent producers in the Milas village purchased yarn and sold carpets through the weaving co-operative in the village. None of these co-operative structures functions as representative organisations of weavers. It is the male heads of households who are the members and weavers do not participate in the co-operative. To the extent that co-operatives are successful in expanding production, facilitating the marketing of carpets and increasing household weaving earnings, they are indirectly beneficial to the weavers in raising and improving their consumption (except when weaving income is directed to meet conspicuous consumption by men). In terms of working conditions and other benefits to weavers, however, the co-operatives do not offer better terms, but adapt to the prevailing conditions in the village. Therefore, an expansion of production is accompanied by intensified working conditions for weavers.

Under the present conditions, the possibility of weavers organising by themselves is limited. Pervasive patriarchal control in the family as well as in the workshop, and lack of paid work alternatives militate against setting up organisations by and for

women. Such an organisational effort can only be realised as part
of a broader government-sponsored rural development programme which
is sensitive to issues of sexual equality. To ensure actual
producers' involvement at the village level, and at the same time
not be a direct threat to men, the collective organisation should
also be designed as a vehicle for extending collective services to
meeting women's needs (such as health care or educational workshops
to familiarise women with techniques which could reduce the drudgery
of the productive and reproductive chores they undertake). In a
setting where men dominate decision-making in all aspects of carpet
production and marketing, the project may never get off the ground
if such organisations are set up with the purpose of transferring
this control to women by excluding men. Thus, the organisation must
encompass a broader but manageable set of objectives that includes
the provision of services to women, to justify as well as encourage
women's participation. The effectiveness of the organisation in
addressing women's needs is crucial to the viability of the organisation in achieving improvements in working conditions and earnings.

Setting up this new collective organisation necessitates the
design and implementation of a unified programme that first of all
requires a restructuring of government activities with respect to
carpet weaving. Unifying and co-ordinating the efforts and pro-
grammes of numerous government agencies under one body is essential
to the success of any effort with respect to carpet weaving. In
addition, this government agency should be charged with setting up
the new type of collective organisation, and overseeing and co-
ordinating the extension of services to women, as well as organising
various aspects of carpet production and marketing.

The proposed organisational effort should be undertaken with
the objective of expanding carpet production under improved conditions of pay and work. The government agency should be charged
with facilitating the achievement of the four goals stated at the
beginning of this section by the village collective organisation.
Specific functions of the agency should be the following:
(a) to offer advice on the most marketable designs and carpet
     types that are likely to command higher unit earnings and
     to make these designs available to village collective organi-
     sations at reasonable prices. This would eliminate the
     dependence of weavers on local dealers or merchants' agents
     for designs and make it possible for weavers to move away
     from weaving carpets that command low unit earnings. It
     would also put an end to the introduction and maintenance of
     regionally based differentials in unit earnings for the same
     types of carpet. For example, the Afyon weavers would not
     need to restrict themselves to weaving the low piece-rate
     carpets for the domestic market put out by Sümberbank, but could
     switch to carpets woven by, for example, the Döşemealtı
     weavers. Similarly, Niğde-1 weavers could have an alternative
     to weaving the type of carpet that is associated with very low
     piece-rates. Through the collective organisation women would

be able to decide on the type of carpet they wished to weave based on unit earnings, knot density and difficulty of design;

(b) to extend credit for looms, construction of workshops and assistance in planning the workshop building so as to facilitate a healthy working environment;

(c) to sell good-quality yarn to the village co-operative. At present, this is the function accomplished by <u>Sümerbank</u> with greatest success;

(d) to inform village collectives of the retail square meter prices for the carpet type they produce as frequently as possible;

(e) to engage in marketing of carpets and to purchase the output of village collectives at prices that are within a reasonable margin of the going retail prices. The government agency could set up domestic marketing outlets but, more important, should attempt to establish itself in the export market. Such an organisational network based on a large number of village-based collective production units has a reasonable chance of succeeding in the export market. At present the primary complaint of exporters is the inadequate supply of carpets of standard sizes and quality, a bottle-neck which an organisational effort on a national and regional scale should have no problem overcoming, whether the marketing is done by the government agency or by exporters;

(f) to extend health and educational services to weavers through joint efforts with the ministries of education and health;

(g) to extend weaving training in regions which lack other income-generating opportunities and where women are not excessively overworked. The study has shown that weaving tends to be a complementary activity, superimposed on existing productive and reproductive tasks of women without any change in the sexual division of labour and without replacing farm activities. This results in a widening of the inequality in the overall workload of men and women. Given this experience, it is important that state policy does not lead to an intensification of women's workload. It is also important to ensure a relatively large carpet output from each collective organisation in order to make the effort worth while. A collective organisation set up in villages of diversified agriculture, often based on heavy use of unpaid family labour, is likely to yield a low carpet output in the relatively short non-agricultural season. It is also likely to be short-lived, especially when the carpet type commands low piece-rates. The Afyon village typifies such a setting, where both the output forthcoming from the co-operative is low and the activity eliminates any leisure time weavers might have. The Konya co-operatives, on the other hand, constitute a successful prototype with regard to the limited income-generating opportunities in the region. Since women in these regions do little agricultural fieldwork, the extension of weaving in this region could also be considered an appropriate strategy (although sexual inequality in the overall workload and poor working conditions in workshops remain a problem);

(h) to teach weaving skills to both men and women. This strategy
     should accompany the two criteria noted above in introducing
     carpet weaving. As noted in the introductory chapter, the
     state policy of extending training only to women has introduced
     or reproduced an idealised and rigid sexual division of labour.
     It is imperative to break the association of weaving with women
     by teaching weaving skills to both boys and girls. This strategy
     would create the possibility for substitution of tasks between
     men and women, and introduce flexibility in the sexual division
     of labour.

The new village collective could be set up under the sponsorship
of the government agency but as an independent organisational structure. The collective should not be obliged to sell its output to the
government agency, provided the going price information is available
to the collective. Training should be extended to develop the
collective structure into a self-governed and self-managed organisation
not dependent on the State. The village collective should be set up
as an alternative to the present system of marketing carpets by
reducing the number of intermediaries between the actual producer and
the consumer. If the intermediate stages in marketing were reduced,
the share of the intermediaries could be channelled to weavers, making
social security coverage and higher earnings possible.

In village collectives, women must be able to make the output
decisions. If workshop organisation is to be continued or re-
organised under the auspices of the collective, then women must make
decisions on working hours and number of breaks during the day, and
must be able to set up flexible work schedules. Alternatively, if
production takes place in homes then the collective could function
as the marketing outlet, as well as the vehicle for purchasing and
distributing the means of production.

The original objectives and functions of Sümerbank and the co-
operatives overlap with the proposed functions to some extent.
However, a number of problems prevent the functioning of the network
to the advantage of weavers and their households. Rigidity of
Sümerbank prices and the agency's lack of dynamism in keeping up
with changing tastes because of its objective of selling to low-
income consumers means that its piece-rates or square meter prices
are outbid by dealers and merchants in the context of market expansion. Thus, the co-operatives have either broken ties with
Sümerbank (Konya-1, 2) or have become defunct, with individual
households becoming dependent on local dealers for marketing, and
vulnerable to the latter's manipulation of prices and piece-rates
(Milas). Others have remained loyal to Sümerbank, which means that
women's work effort continues to be valued at very low piece-rates
(Afyon).

Besides the proposed organisational effort, legislative and
enforcement measures must be undertaken to improve working conditions
in workshops and to make possible the extension of social benefits to
weavers. Enacting special legislation governing hours, the physical
condition of workshops and social benefits could be one way of
confronting these problems. Even if no new legislation governing

92

the carpet industry is enacted, serious efforts must be made to
enforce social security coverage in workshops. In addition, the
SSL must be revised to make possible the extension of some form of
benefits to home weavers and to the youngest workshop weavers
(below the age of 16). The revised or newly designed social benefits
plan must also make access to coverage relatively easy, and not
create too much paperwork. It must appeal to those covered whether
they be home or workshop weavers. It must also appear as less of a
burden to the employer than the present law, so that it will put an
end to the alleged bribery of the social security inspectors.

Legislation alone would not ensure the improvement in working
conditions, however. Given the scattered nature of employment and
the dependence of a considerable number of households on weaving
income, it would be very difficult to ensure employers' compliance.
A formidable obstacle in improving working conditions, providing
weavers with long-term social benefits and enhancing their autonomy
is the inability of weavers to voice their demands, given the com-
plicity of men with employers and the divisions among weavers themselves. However, if enforcement accompanies the proposed organisational changes towards minimising intermediation in marketing, a
reasonable measure of success in the extension of benefits can be
expected. Even if it only serves as a frame of reference, the
importance of legislation cannot be minimised.

These legislative and organisational changes must be accompanied
by a general educational programme, which among other things is
designed to create and reinforce more positive gender roles for women.
The present narrow range of roles projected in the media does not
leave much room for changes in traditional gender roles in rural
Turkish society. In the context of a lack of positive identities
to which women can aspire, efforts to wrest some of men's entrenched
control over decision-making is seen to breed immorality and dis-
obedience, attributes which rural women do not wish to be accused of.

APPENDIX I

RESEARCH METHODOLOGY

    The selection of the weaving regions in the study is based on
information obtained from carpet importers in the United States, and
exporters, merchants and civil servants in Turkey. The primary consideration in the selection of weaving regions was that they should
be representative of different groups of carpets produced in rural
Turkey today. Such groups are identified by type of market, pattern
and knot density per square area of carpet. Given the close
association of carpet groups with the relations under which they are
produced, the representativeness of type of carpet to a large extent
implies representativeness in relations of production in carpet
weaving. The representativeness achieved is not statistical, but
only illustrative, however, in view of the small number of case
studies against the background of the decentralised structure of the
industry. Moreover, while efforts were made to include weaving
regions of major carpet groups in the study, the regions included
in the study do not exhaust the major carpet groups produced in
Turkey today.

    After the weaving regions were determined, an attempt was made
to select a representative village in each in terms of land tenure
system, crops, the extent of agricultural mechanisation and integration into the national commodity and labour markets. Selection
of the actual case study villages depended on the ability to
establish a connection in a village in the region identified, and
was not based on an a priori analysis of secondary sources. This
was due to the lack of regional and village level studies and for
practical reasons. People from various backgrounds - civil servants,
merchants, friends and first-generation migrants from rural areas -
helped set up contacts that led to the villages. Despite difficulties, we believe that the case studies selected illustrate production relations in carpet weaving in Turkey and of agriculture in
the regions in question.

    The outcome of the case study selection methodology was a wide
variation in various demographic and economic characteristics, which
posed difficulties in the formulation of a structured questionnaire
that would be applicable to all contexts, and yet be capable of
gathering the basic quantifiable information needed. In order to
test and refine the research method, three pilot case studies were
undertaken. The Afyon and Niğde-1 villages were selected for the

initial pilot studies. The Afyon study was exploratory, heavily
relying on open-ended interviews during a week's stay. In the
Niğde-1 village, in three weeks different drafts of the questionnaire.
were tested in addition to open-ended and group interviews with
weavers.

The third pilot case study was conducted in Hereke, the traditional centre of silk carpet weaving, in the industrialised Marmara
region near Istanbul. Although not a rural area, the Hereke study
provided valuable insights for later village case studies. As a
town where the putting-out system, workshop production and independent
production co-exist, Hereke offered the opportunity to study the
conditions under different relations of production. Moreover, the
Hereke study made possible the examination of the employment impact of
rapid changes in carpet demand, since Hereke had experienced a growth
of the market in the late 1970s followed by a contraction in the early
1980s. In Hereke, open-ended interviews were conducted with
Sümerbank managers, merchants and workshop owners, as well as
structured interviews with weavers who wove under different relations
of production.

After the Hereke study, the final form of the questionnaire
was administered in the remaining and pilot case study villages.
Following initial trips to the case study villages and a preliminary
evaluation of the data collected, second field trips to each village
were made. Thereby, lacunae or inconsistencies in the information
collected were checked, issues were further explored and new interviews conducted. In each case study village the author spent a total
of approximately two weeks, except for the Niğde-1 village (one
month).

The research relied primarily on a questionnaire, and on open-
ended and group interviews with weavers. The questionnaire was
rarely administered through the open use of the questionnaire form.
Interviews combined open-ended discussion with questions from the
questionnaire, and responses were later recorded in the questionnaire. Since the study did not benefit from any background studies
on weaving or the agrarian structure in the regions and villages
selected, inquiries were necessary regarding the development of
carpet weaving in the area, and changes in both the economic structure
of the village and women's position. Thus, in each village discussions with several villagers and the agricultural extension agent
were conducted. In addition, open-ended interviews with merchants,
organisers of production and village dealers at different levels in
the hierarchy of the industry in each region were the major source
of information on the history and present structure of the carpet
industry.

APPENDIX II

MEASUREMENT OF HOUSEHOLD INCOME

In the calculation of household income, the reference period was the 12 months prior to the date of the interview. Since the research extended through a ten-month period, it was not possible to have a standard reference period for each weaver in the sample, which posed difficulties in calculation of incomes. The problem was remedied through second field trips when the information was brought up to date. When it was not possible to interview the same weavers on second field visits, 1983 price averages for each village were used in the calculation of household earnings and costs of production, along with the corresponding quantities declared in the initial interview. Total household income, which is the net income of co-resident family members, was calculated as follows:

Total household income = farm income (crop and animal production) + weaving income + rental income + wage income + commerce income + other income.

Non-weaving income

Most of the data needed to calculate non-weaving income components of household income were obtained through the survey questionnaire. The questionnaire was designed to capture only partial information needed for the calculation of net earnings from sources other than weaving. Two considerations were relevant in not including a standard set of questions on non-weaving sources of income: (a) the diversity of sources of income across villages and the particular cost structure relevant to each would have made the design of a standard questionnaire a cumbersome enterprise; (b) if detailed questions on the costs of production had been included, in cases where the questionnaire was inspected by the male relative of the weaver, it would most certainly have raised suspicions about the purpose of the study. Suspicion of a possible use of information for tax purposes would have jeopardised the reliability of responses not only to these questions but also to the rest.

Farm income

This was calculated on the basis of questionnaire information on gross earnings from the production of subsistence and cash crops on land held in usufruct by co-resident family members, as well as from the sale of animals. During interviews the questionnaire was supplemented by another set of questions asked in an open-ended format to capture information on the amount of inputs by each household in agricultural and animal production. Where applicable, questions on animal products were also added during the interview. This information was supplemented by and checked against information on costs of production (unit input use and unit price of each input) obtained from the agricultural extension officer of the village or nearby town, as well as from male farmers.

Wage income

This represents total cash and (monetised) in-kind returns from non-weaving work performed by household members, from which cash and in-kind payments to others for work performed is deducted.

Rental income

This includes cash and in-kind rental income from share-croppers net of rent payments to landowners for use of land.

Commerce and other income

This category was calculated on the basis of information obtained in open-ended discussions. The listing of occupations of household members provided an opportunity to obtain information on monthly, daily or unit earnings as well as the length of time worked or units produced in commerce and other self-employment activities. Annual income based on the minimum wage was used as a yardstick in estimating income from commerce and transport. In a few cases, where a household member was away at work, the amount of remittances was either asked about directly or was estimated on the basis of the monthly income of the migrant. Likewise, cash or in-kind contributions by kin to the household were also recorded. Inevitably, the calculation of income from petty commerce or irregular work contains imperfections. Yet a reasonable effort was made to capture the requisite information on which the estimation was based.

Measurement of weaving output

In the survey, information on weaving output was collected in terms of number of carpets of various sizes and knot densities. A square meter measure of carpet output could not be adopted, however, due to differences in knot densities (the number of knots per 100 square centimetres). In order to obtain a comparable standard whereby earnings and productivity differentials across the sample could be analysed, the raw output data contained in questionnaires had to be translated into number of knots. This translation may contain inaccuracies, but is defensible on the grounds that any inaccuracies will tend to be consistent throughout the sample and, given the nature of the product, this is the only plausible method of measuring weaving output.

To measure the weaving output of each weaver accurately, during fieldwork either the knot density and dimensions of each carpet were measured, or the declared dimensions of each carpet and its number of warp strings and rows of knots were recorded. In the event that the requisite information for estimating knot density could not be obtained during a particular interview, then the knot density of carpets of similar design and size woven by another household in the same village was used as a proxy.

Where more than one weaver worked at a loom, individual output was calculated by dividing the total number of knots by the number of weavers. In the case of independent weavers, the calculation of household carpet output was straightforward since the number of carpets woven by household members is the same as those woven by the principal weaver. In the case of workshop weavers, however, the total number of carpets produced by household members was computed on the basis of the principal weaver's output. The potential inaccuracy in the imputation of the weaving output of other household members was remedied during the interview by trying to capture information on the extent to which other household weavers wove during the reference period.

Calculation of weaving income

Calculation of the weaving earnings of the principal weaver involved a number of steps. Total earnings of workshop weavers and outworkers were recorded in net terms and were derived from the total number of knots tied at the weighted average wage per 1,000 knots during the reference period. For independent weavers, on the other hand, total earnings based on the number of carpets sold at given prices represented gross earnings only, except for carpets produced on order of customers. Thus, for independent weavers costs of production were deducted in order to arrive at net revenues.

The total cost of production incurred by the independent weavers consisted of monetary expenditures by the household on carpets produced. For those households where labour is expended in all stages of the preparation of yarn from wool, monetary costs do not reflect the cost of production fully, however. In order to remedy this underestimation, in the calculation of total cost of production incurred by the households that have spun the yarn from wool, the average cost of production based on market prices of machine-spun yarn was used.

A second complication in the calculation of net weaving income arises because some independent producers do not sell the carpets immediately or during the course of the reference period. The actual net weaving income of these households was lower than it would have been had they sold all their output. Adopting a potential income definition, the weaving earnings in the study are calculated as if all independent producer households had sold all the carpets they produced during the reference period.

The first step in the calculation of weaving income was the calculation of unit earnings from weaving. The 1,000-knot wage, which is the conventional piece-rate basis used in merchant-controlled weaving, was adopted as the measure of unit earnings for all weavers in this study. This required the calculation of earnings per 1,000 knots for independent producers, who are paid a per carpet sum regardless of the knot count of the carpet. Moreover, unit earnings of outworkers and workshop weavers who are paid in terms of 1,000-knot wages had to be recalculated to reflect accurately changes in the piece-rate during the fieldwork period. The average piece-rate was weighted both by the number of months different piece-rates prevailed in the village and by the piece-rate applicable to each weaver, thereby taking into consideration the seasonal concentration of her weaving activity or distribution of the number of knots tied by each weaver across the reference period.

QUESTIONNAIRE FOR THE SURVEY OF RURAL CARPET WEAVERS

Date: ....   Province: ....
                          Town : ....
                          Village: ....

A. Household composition

Name	Relation-ship to weaver	Sex	Age	Marital status	Educa-tion	Principal* occupa-tion	Secondary* occupa-tion
1.							
2.							
3.							
4.							
5.							
6.							
7.							
8.							
9.							

* If different from agriculture, include estimated earnings per month, day or unit.

B. Questions on carpet weaving

1. At what age did you start weaving? ....

2. Who taught you how to weave?
    Mother 1   Other relative 2   Neighbour 3   Teacher 4

3. Where do you presently weave?
    At home 1   At a workshop 2

3a. Where did you learn weaving?
    At home 1   At a workshop 2

4. Whom do you weave with?   Alone 1   With another weaver 2

4a. <u>Relationship   Age   Always   Sometimes   Rarely</u>

    1.
    2.
    3.
    4.

5. On the days that you weave, how many hours do you weave?

    Schedule: Total number of hours:

If she weaves at home:

6. Which members of the household undertake the following tasks
   and at what frequency?

    Washing wool 1   Dyeing 6
    Spinning wool 2   Setting up warp 7
    Washing yarn 3   Weaving 8
    Making skeins 4   Other 9
    Making balls 5

    <u>Always   Sometimes   Rarely   Never   Not applicable</u>

    1.
    2.
    3.
    4.

7. Whom do you weave for?

    Merchant 1   On own account 2   Co-operative 3

7a. For how many years now? ..... years   .... months

7b. Whom did you weave for before?

Order in time	Employer*	Labour process**	Length of time	Reasons for change
1.				
2.				
3.				
4.				

* Merchant 1   ** Home   1
  On own account 2   Workshop 2
  Co-operative 3
  Did not weave 4
  For use 5

If she weaves for someone else:

8. What does this person provide you with?

    Loom 1   Design 6
    Yarn 2   Scissors 7
    Dyed yarn 3   Knife 8
    Wool 4   Comb 9
    Dye 5   Other 10

9. Does this person give you advances? Yes 1   No 2

9a. Did you get an advance this year? Yes 1 No 2   Amount: .....

9b. Had you received an advance before? Yes 1   No 2

10. Information on carpets woven in the last 12 months:

Type	Type I	Type II	Type III
Knot density per 100 cm^2			
Dimensions			
Number of carpets			
Number of weavers			
Length of time*			
I.			
II.			
Per carpet earnings			
Wage/1,000 knots			
Total earnings			
Total m^2			

*I - Actual
 II - Shortest possible length of time

11. How many carpets did you weave in the previous year?

    About the same 1   Less 2   More 3

11a. Reason(s) for difference:

    Health reasons 1   Assistance 2   Need for income 3 Other 4

If she weaves on own account:

12. Cost of production of these carpets:

TL/kg*	Type I kg cost	Type II kg cost	Type III kg cost
Warp yarn			
Weft yarn			
Knot yarn			
Cost of yarn			
Cost of dyes			
Other expenses			
....			
....			
Per carpet cost			
Total cost			

*On credit - V; Down-payment price - P.

13. Where do you sell these carpets? ....

14. Who sells them? ....

15. Do you sell the carpet immediately after the weaving is completed?

Yes 1   No 2

15a. Why? ....

16. How is the payment made?

Cash 1   In kind 2   Both 3

16a. If cash:

Down payment 1   Term payment 2   Both 3

17. Who receives the payment? Myself 1   Someone else 2 ....

C. Work alternatives

18. Do you work at other jobs besides carpet weaving?

Yes 1 (Go to 18a)
No 2 (Go to 18b)

18a. What type of work? ....

Length of time devoted: .... Wage: ....
Since when? ....
Do you prefer weaving or this job? ....

18b. Why?

There are no jobs available	1
I am not allowed to work at another job	2
I cannot because of my young children	3
I cannot because of health reasons	4
My domestic responsibilities are many	5
Other:	6

19.   Would you like to have worked at another job rather than weave?

Yes 1 (Go to 19a)
No   2 (Go to 19c)

19a. What kind of a job? ....

19b. Why don't you? ....

19c. Why? ....
....

20.   Would you like to weave at home or in a workshop? ....

20a. Why? ....

21.   Tell me the economic activities you engage in throughout the year: (last 12 months)

September
October
November
December
January
February
March
April
May
June
July
August

D.   Use of income

22.   What do you usually spend weaving income on?

Foodstuffs	1	Dowry spending	5
Clothing	2	Agricultural expenses	6
Education	3	Agricultural invest-	
Consumer durables	4	ment	7
		Other:	8

23. What are you going to buy with your next payment of weaving earnings?

   ....

24. Do you keep cash?   Yes 1   No 2

24a. For what purpose? ....

25. Do you go shopping?   Yes 1   No 2

25a. If she goes shopping:

Location	Alone*	Purpose	Frequency
In the village 1			
Closest town 2			
Provincial centre 3			

   *Yes 1   No 2

26. Can your household subsist without weaving income?

   We could do without it   1
   It would be difficult   2
   We cannot subsist   3

27. If we order the incomes of your household, how would they rank from largest to smallest?

   1.
   2.
   3.
   4.

E.   Household's economic position

28. Do you own land?   Yes 1   No 2   Amount: ....

29. If you cultivate land, what are the crops and the amount of land you have cultivated in the last 12 months?

Crop	Amount of land cultivated	Form of land use*	Level of production	For the market**	Unit price	Total earnings
1.						
2.						
3.						
4.						
5.						
6.						
7.						

```
*Given to share-cropper        1        ** Yes  1     No  2
 Taken from owner to share-
    crop                        2
 Own land                      3
 Rented out by household       4
 Rented by household           5
```

30. Rental income/cost: ....

In the last 12 months:

	Task	Number of persons/Who in the household	Number of days	Payment

31. Did you hire wage labour?

Yes 1   No 2

32. Did you work in return for wages?

Yes 1   No 2

33. Did you work in return for payment in kind?

Yes 1   No 2

34. Did you engage in labour exchange?

Yes 1   No 2

35. Agricultural means of production owned by the household: ....
....
Form of use: ....

36. Do you own animals? Yes 1   No 2

36a. Type and number of animals owned by the household: ....
....

37. Have you sold any animals in the past 12 months? Yes 1   No 2

37a. Reason: .... Earnings: ....

BIBLIOGRAPHY

Abadan-Unat, Nermin (ed.). 1981. Women in Turkish society. Leiden, Brill.

Arizpe, Lourdes; Aranda, Josefina. 1981. "The 'comparative advantages' of women's disadvantages: Women workers in strawberry export agribusiness in Mexico", in Signs (Chicago), winter, 7, pp. 453-473.

Ayata, Sencer. 1982. Differentiation and capital accumulation: Case studies of the carpet and metal industries in Kayseri (Turkey). Unpublished Ph.D. thesis. Canterbury, University of Kent, Department of Sociology and Social Anthropology.

Balaman, Ali Rıza. 1985. "Family formation and dissolution in rural areas", in Erder, Türköz (ed.). Family in Turkish society: Sociological and legal studies. Ankara, Turkish Social Science Association.

Barrett, Michele. 1980. Women's oppression today. London, Verso and NLB.

Benería, Lourdes. 1979. "Reproduction, production and the sexual division of labor", in Cambridge Journal of Economics (London), Sep., pp. 203-225.

---. 1982. "Accounting for women's work", in idem (ed.). Women and development: The sexual division of labor in rural societies. New York, Praeger.

---; Sen, Gita. 1982. "Class and gender inequalities and women's role in economic development: Theoretical and practical implications", in Feminist Studies (Maryland), spring, pp. 157-177.

Berik, Günseli. 1986. Women's employment in handwoven carpet production in rural Turkey. Unpublished Ph.D. thesis. Amherst, University of Massachusetts, Department of Economics.

Celbiş, Feridun. 1979. "El dokuma halıcılığının kırsal alan kalkınmasındaki önemi ve üreticilerin örgütlenmesi" [The importance of handwoven carpet production in rural development and the organisation of producers], in Türk El Dokuma Halıcılığı Semineri [Seminar on Turkish handwoven carpet production]. Ankara, Sümerbank.

Deere, Carmen Diana; Leon de Leal, Magdalena. 1982. Women in Andean agriculture. Geneva, ILO.

de Janvry, Alain. 1981. The agrarian question and reformism in Latin America. Baltimore and London, Johns Hopkins University Press.

Dixon, Ruth. 1981. "Jobs for women in rural industry and services", in Lewis, Barbara C. (ed.). Invisible farmers: Women and the crisis in agriculture. Washington, DC, Office of Women in Development, AID.

Devlet Planlama Teşkilatı (DPT). 1966. İkinci Beş yıllık kalkınma planı, dokuma ve giyim sektörü, özel ihtisas komisyonu raporu: Halıcılık alt komisyon raporu [Second five-year plan, textile and apparel industry, special commission report: Carpet weaving subcommittee report]. Yayın No. DPT: 411-ÖİK: 45, Ankara.

---. 1972. Üçüncü beş yıllık kalkınma planı, dokuma ve giyim sektörü, özel ihtisas komisyonu raporu: Halıcılık alt komisyon raporu [Third five-year plan, textile and apparel industry, special commission report: Carpet weaving subcommittee report]. Yayın No. DPT: 1187-ÖİK: 153, Ankara.

---. 1976. Dördüncü beş yıllık kalkınma planı, dokuma ve giyim sektörü, özel ihtisas komisyonu raporu: Halıcılık alt komisyon raporu [Fourth five-year plan, textile and apparel industry, special commission report: Carpet weaving subcommittee report]. Yayın No. DPT: 1515-ÖİK: 213, Ankara.

---. 1982. Beşinci beş yıllık kalkınma planı, dokuma ve giyim sektörü, özel ihtisas komisyonu raporu: Halıcılık alt komisyon raporu [Fifth five-year plan, textile and apparel industry, special commission report: Carpet weaving subcommittee report]. Ankara. Mimeographed.

Durusel, Vedat. 1983. El halıcılığımızın dünya pazarlarında dünü, bugünü ve yarını [Past, present and future of Turkish carpet weaving in world markets]. Istanbul.

Dwyer, Daisy Hilse. 1978. Images and self-images: Male and female in Morocco. New York, Columbia University Press.

Elson, Diane; Pearson, Ruth. 1981. "The subordination of women and the internationalization of factory production", in Young, Kate; Wolkowitz, Carol; McCullagh, Roslyn (eds.). Of marriage and the market. London, Conference of Socialist Economists.

ILO. 1982. Rural women workers in Asia, Report on a Workshop at the ILO International Centre for Advanced Technical and Vocational Training, Turin, Italy, Nov.-Dec. 1981. Geneva.

Kağıtçıbaşı, Çiğdem (ed.). 1982. Sex roles, family and community in Turkey. Indiana, Indiana University, Turkish Studies Department.

110

Kandiyoti, Deniz. 1984. "Rural transformation in Turkey and its implications for women's status", in UNESCO. Women on the move: Contemporary changes in family and society. Paris.

Longhurst, Richard. 1982. "Resource allocation and sexual division of labor: A case study of a Moslem Hausa village in northern Nigeria", in Beneria, Lourdes. (ed.). Women and development: The sexual division of labor in rural societies. New York, Praeger/ILO.

Mies, Maria. 1982. "The dynamics of the sexual division of labor and integration of rural women into the world market", ibid.

Ozbay, Ferhunde. 1982. "Women's education in rural Turkey", in Çiğdem Kağıtçıbaşı (ed.). Sex roles, family and community in Turkey. Indiana, Indiana University, Turkish Studies Department.

---. 1985. "Transformation of the socioeconomic structure and changing family functions in rural Turkey", in Erder, Türköz (ed.). Family in Turkish society: Sociological and legal studies. Ankara, Turkish Social Science Association.

Özden, Lütfi. 1979. "Türkiye'de halı üretiminin yaygınlaştırılması" [Expansion of carpet production in Turkey], in Türk El Dokuma Halıcılığı Semineri [Seminar on Turkish handwoven carpet production]. Ankara, Sümerbank.

Quataert, Donald. 1986. "Machine breaking and the changing carpet industry of western Anatolia, 1860-1908" in Journal of Social History (Pittsburgh), spring, pp. 473-490.

Quinn, Naomi. 1977. "Anthropological studies on women's status", in Siegel, Bernard J.; Beals, Alan R.; Tyler, Stephen A. (eds.). Annual review of anthropology. Palo Alto, Annual Reviews Inc., pp. 181-222.

Roldán, Martha. 1985. "Industrial outworking, struggles for reproduction of working class families and gender subordination", in Redclift, Nanneke; Mingione, Enzo (eds.). Beyond employment. Oxford, Basil Blackwell.

Safilios-Rothschild, Constantina. 1982. "Female power, autonomy and demographic change in the Third World", in Anker, Richard; Buvinic, Mayra; Youssef, Nadia H. (eds.). Women's roles and population trends in the Third World. London, ILO/Croom Helm.

State Institute of Statistics (SIS). 1982. 1980 Population census 1 per cent sample results. Ankara.

---. 1983. 1980 Agricultural Survey. Ankara.

Stoler, Ann. 1977. "Class structure and female autonomy in rural Java", in Wellesley Editorial Collective (ed.). Women and national development: The complexities of change. Chicago and London, University of Chicago Press.

Timur, Serim. 1981. "Determinants of family structure in Turkey", in Abadan-Unat, op. cit.

Türkiye Ticaret Odaları, Sanayi Odaları ve Ticaret Borsaları Birliği. 1959. Türkiye'de halıcılık [Carpet weaving in Turkey]. Ankara.

Ülker, Taha. 1979. "Makina halıcılığının teşvikinin el halıcılığına dolaylı etkileri [Indirect effects of promotion of machine-woven carpet production on handwoven carpet production]", in Türk El Dokuma Halıcılığı Semineri [Seminar on Turkish handwoven carpet production]. Ankara, Sümerbank.

Whyte, Martin King. 1978. The status of women in pre-industrial societies. Princeton, Princeton University Press.

Young, Kate. 1978. "Modes of appropriation and the sexual division of labour: A case study from Oaxaca, Mexico", in Kuhn, Annette; Wolpe, Annmarie (eds.). Feminism and materialism. London, Routledge and Kegan Paul.

Youssef, Nadia; Hetler, Carol B. 1983. "Establishing the economic condition of women-headed households in the Third World: A new approach", in Buvinic, Mayra; Lycette, Margaret A.; McGreevey, William Paul (eds.). Women and poverty in the Third World. Baltimore and London, Johns Hopkins University Press.

Women, Work and Development

(ISSN 0253-2042) – Some earlier titles in the series

Unpaid work in the household: A review of economic evaluation methods,
by Luisella Goldschmidt-Clermont   WWD 1

This monograph examines the various economic approaches used to evaluate unpaid work in the household. Herein lies its originality. It analyses the strengths and weaknesses of each method, particularly in relation to social values and labour market conditions. The monograph provides a useful starting-point in a field deserving further investigation, both in developed countries and, subject to testing and adapting methodologies as appropriate, in the developing world as well.   17.50 Sw. frs.   ISBN 92-2-103085-7

From peasant girls to Bangkok masseuses, by Pasuk Phongpaichit   WWD 2

Peasant girls living in poor regions of northern and north-eastern Thailand are drawn to the capital, Bangkok, to earn a living through prostitution. This monograph looks at this well-known and flourishing trade from the point of view of the masseuse girls themselves, whose attitude is predominantly one of resignation.   15 Sw. frs.   ISBN 92-2-103013-X

State policies and the position of women workers in the People's Democratic Republic of Yemen, 1967-77, by Maxine Molyneux   WWD 3

This monograph, which is the first survey of women in Democratic Yemen, analyses the main changes that have occurred in the position of women as a result of state policies and economic development, and discusses the measures implemented by the State as regards women's legal status, their political involvement, their education and their employment.
                              17.50 Sw. frs.   ISBN 92-2-103144-6

Women in Andean agriculture: Peasant production and rural wage employment in Colombia and Peru, by Carmen Diana Deere and Magdalena León de Leal WWD 4

According to the prevailing interpretation of census data, the Andean region of South America has a male farming system. This monograph challenges that interpretation by showing that rural women participate actively in agriculture, both within peasant units of production and in the rural labour force. Census data suggest that the participation of rural women in agriculture has decreased in recent decades; but the findings of this monograph imply that it may in fact be increasing, both within smallholder production and in the seasonal agricultural wage labour force.   20 Sw. frs.   ISBN 92-2-103106-3

Women workers in the Sri Lanka plantation sector: An historical and contemporary analysis, by Rachel Kurian   WWD 5

Plantation labour systems display certain similarities across regions, cultures and crops, and they have some common historical roots. Commonly, too, the position of women workers in agriculture in many countries is unfavourable. In this monograph the author, on the basis of her field research, traces the particular evolution of the plantation system in Sri Lanka and portrays the nature and conditions of work by women on tea, rubber and coconut plantations. Suggestions are made for improvement. 20 Sw. frs.   ISBN 92-2-102992-1

Fertility, female employment and policy measures in Hungary,
by Barnabás Barta, András Klinger, Károly Miltényi and György Vukovich   WWD 6

Has women's employment in fact been an important factor affecting fertility? Are there other factors and policies contributing to lower fertility? These and other questions are examined in this detailed study of Hungary, which not only gives demographic and employment data for the Hungarian population as a whole but also provides interesting information on KAP (Knowledge, Attitude and Practice of Family Planning) surveys, panel surveys of marriage cohorts, and time budget studies.   15 Sw. frs.   ISBN 92-2-103624-3

Craftswomen in Kerdassa, Egypt: Household production and reproduction,
by Patricia D. Lynch with Hoda Fahmy   WWD 7

This monograph describes the contributions of women in an Egyptian community to subsistence activities and handicrafts production, and the changes in labour processes which increasingly push women into less rewarding forms of work. It discusses the ways in which women's work is related to child-bearing and rearing and the significance of children's work for increased productivity.   15 Sw. frs.   ISBN 92-2-103625-1